LYNNE PICKERING

OUTSIDER ART & INTERIORS

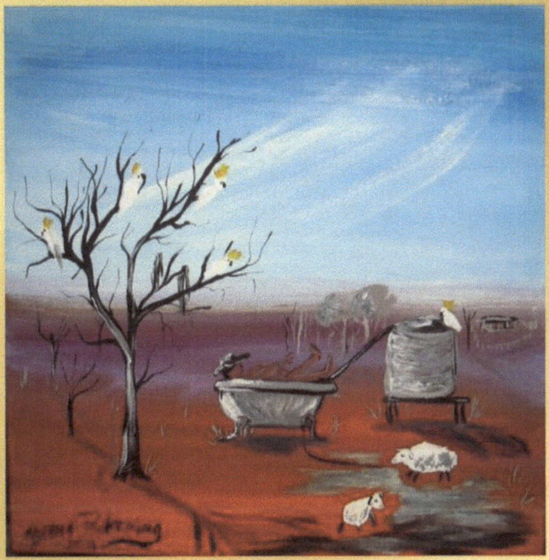

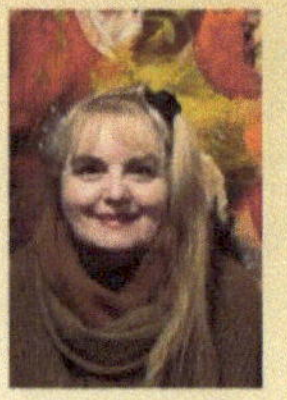

ISBN 13:978-1517121266

ISBN 10: 1517121264

CREATE SPACE PLATFORM

DEDICATION

I want to thank my husband for packing 5,500 paintings sold over thirty two countries without his help this would not have been possible.

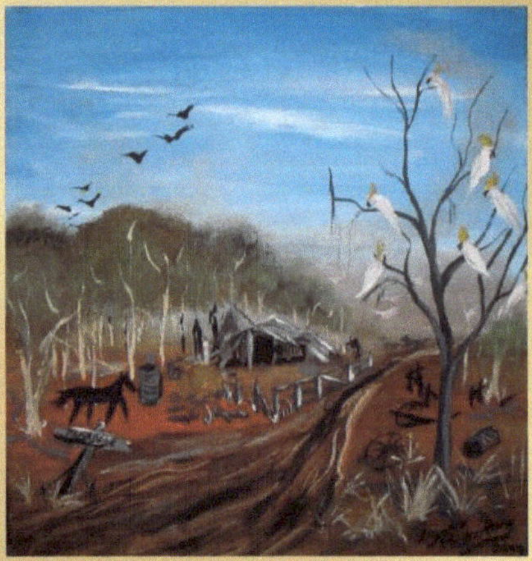

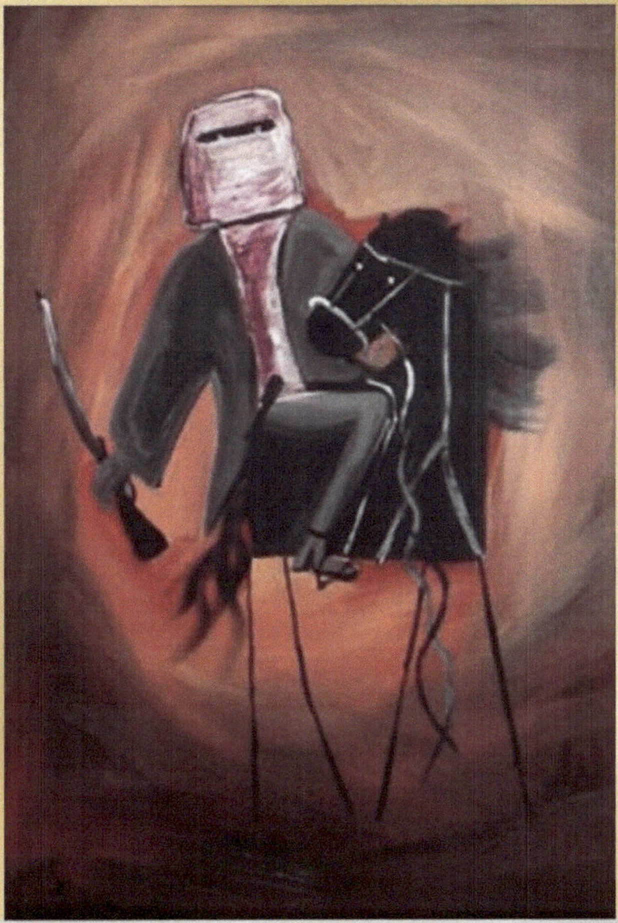

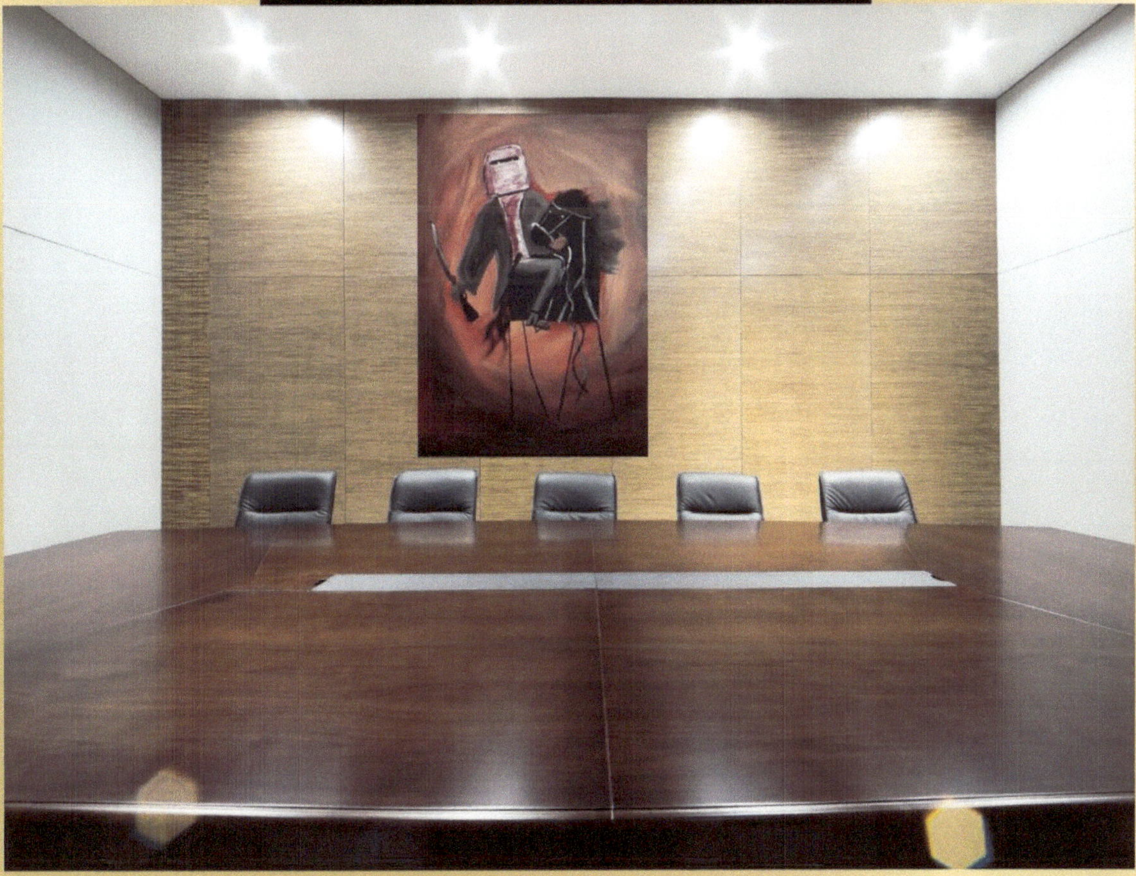

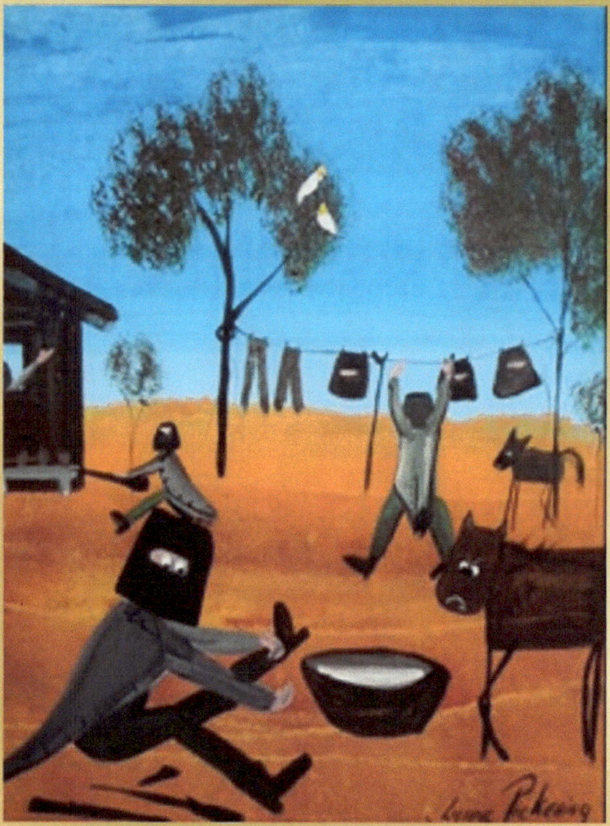

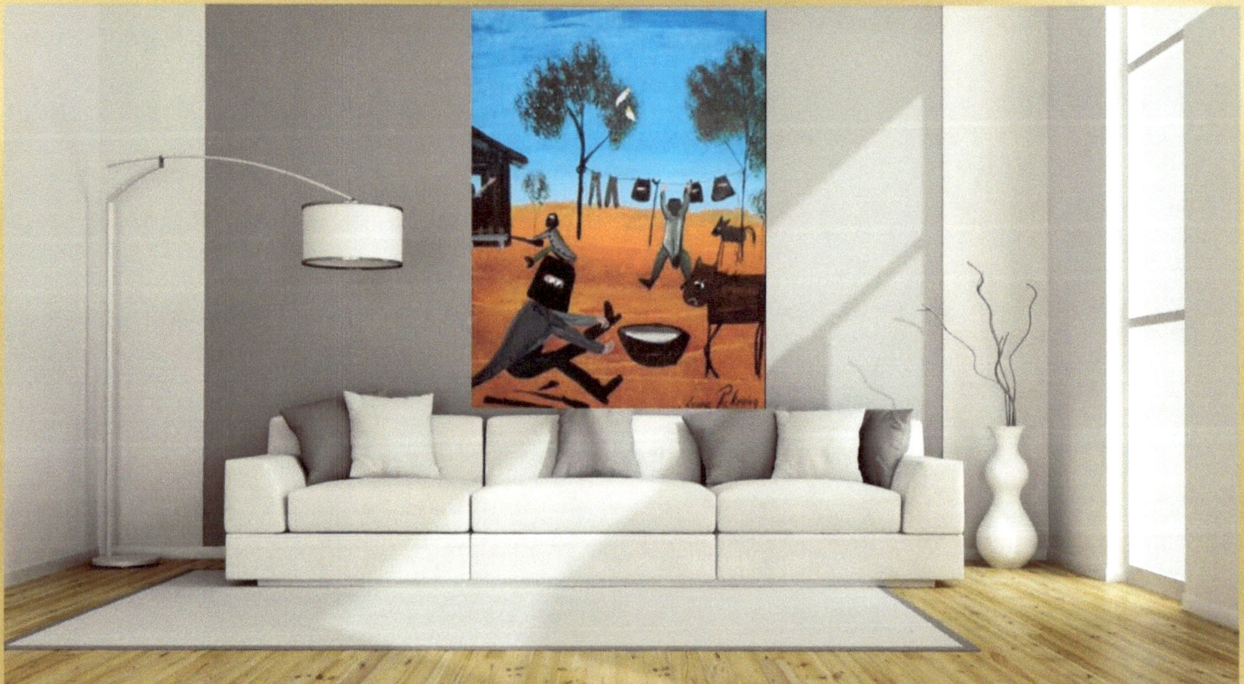

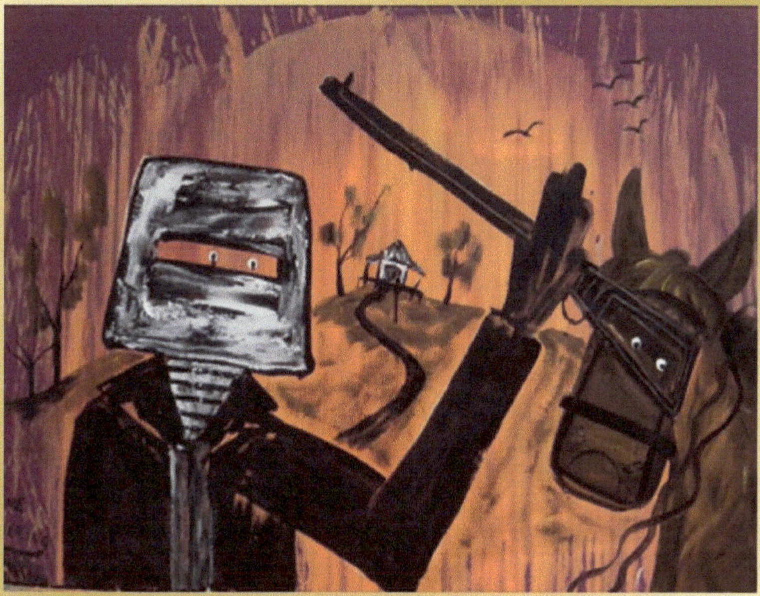

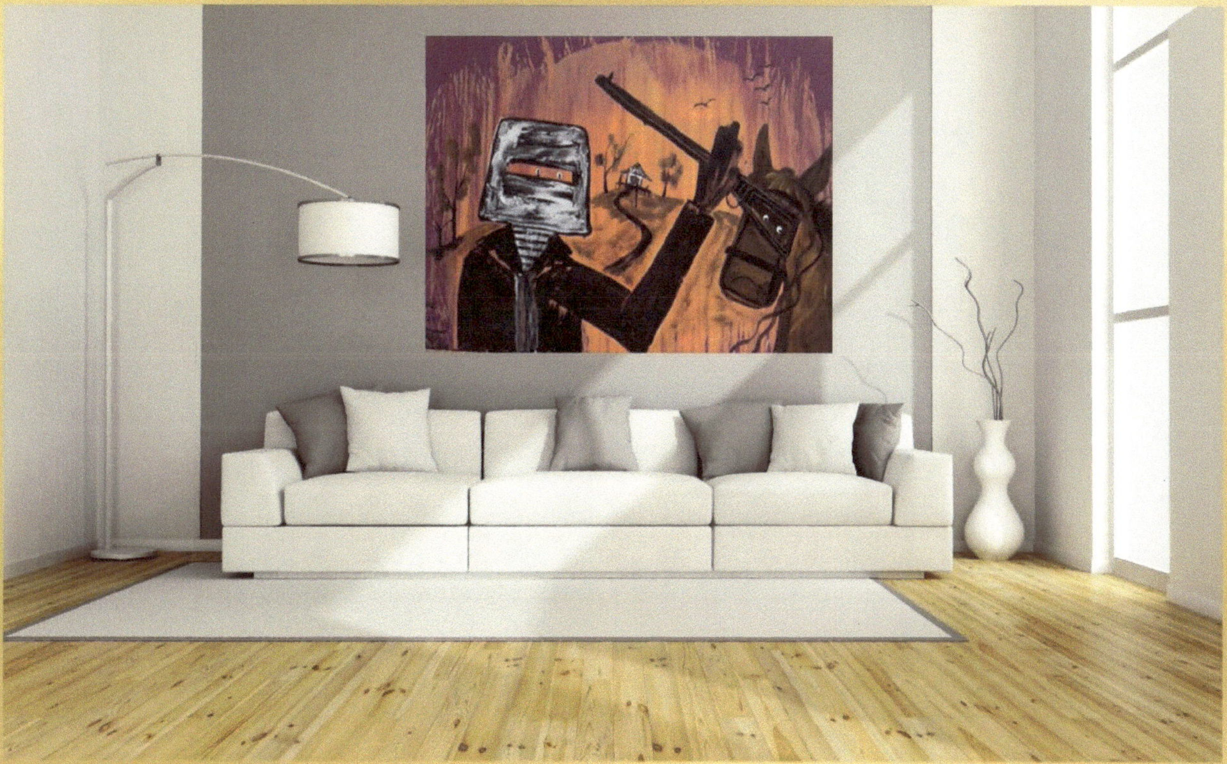

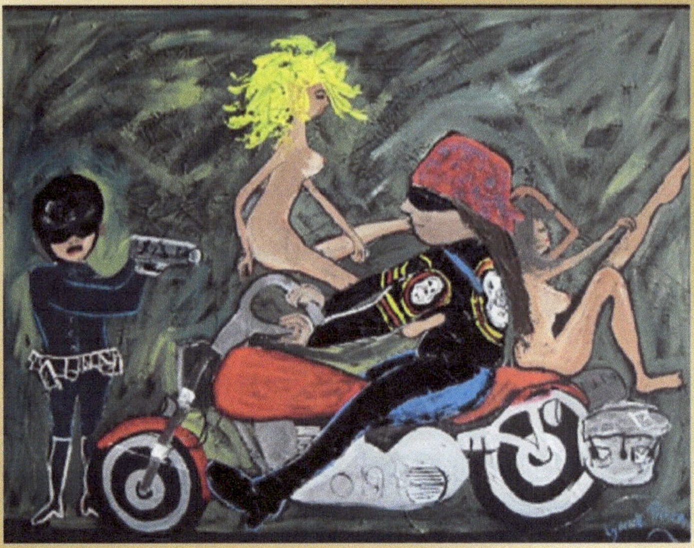

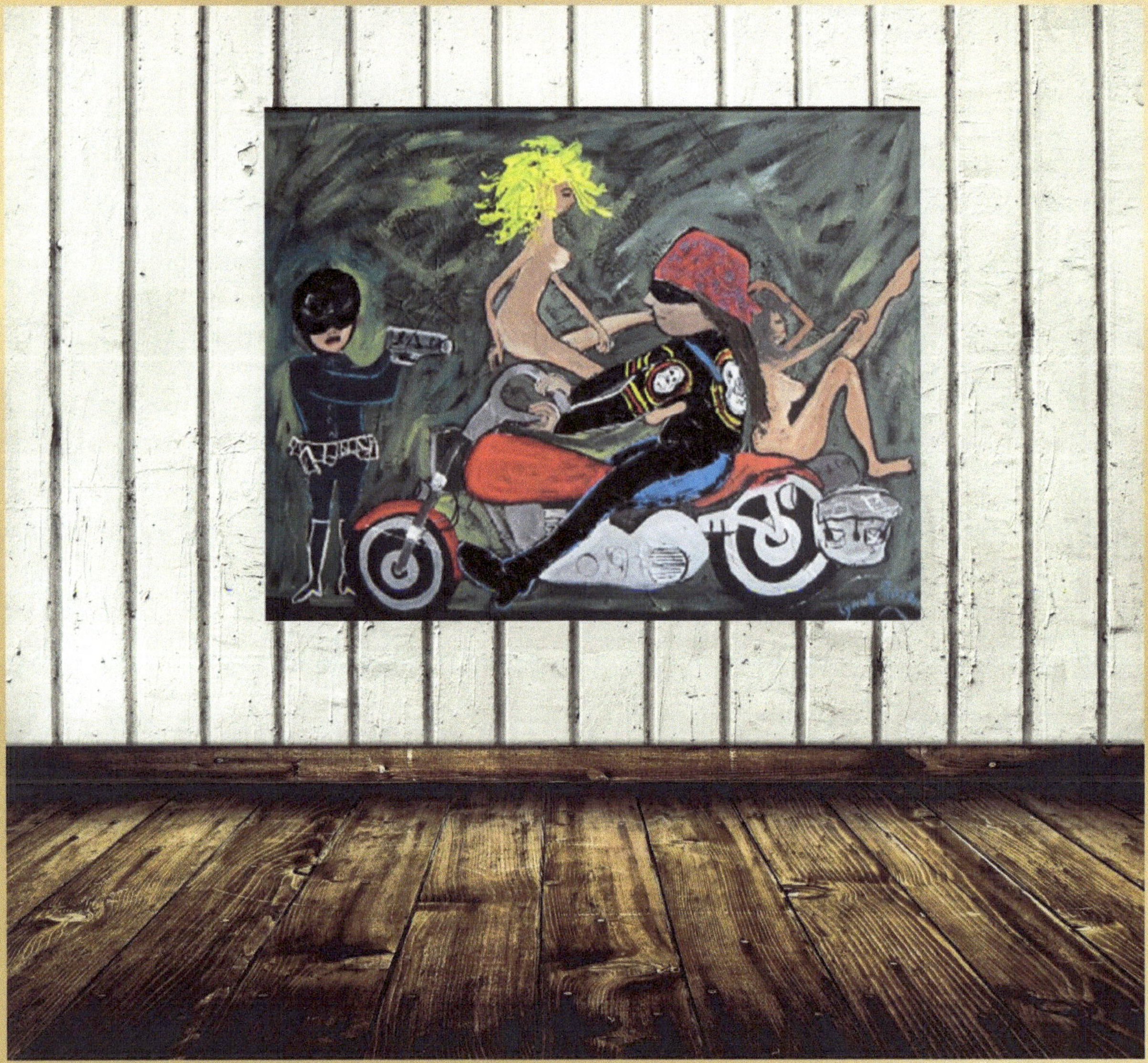

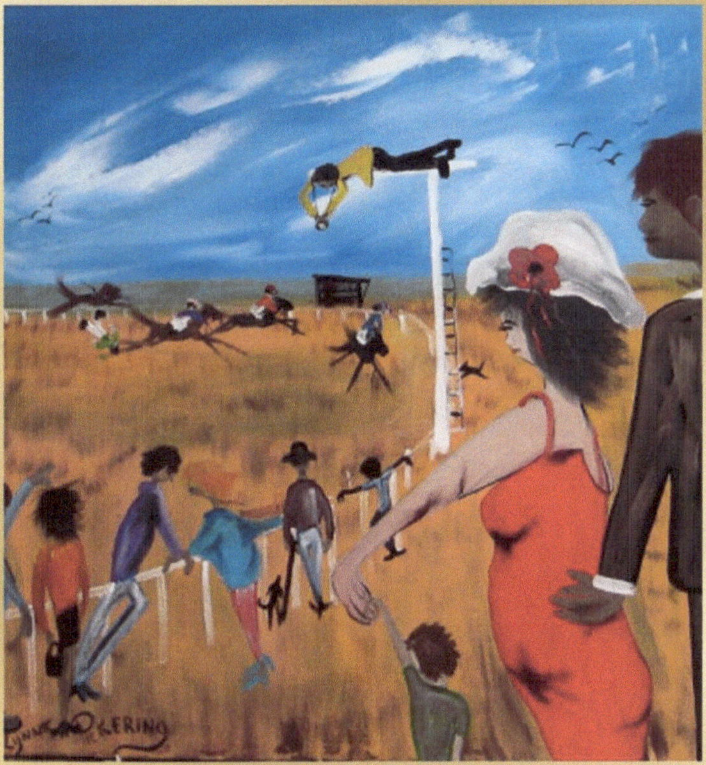

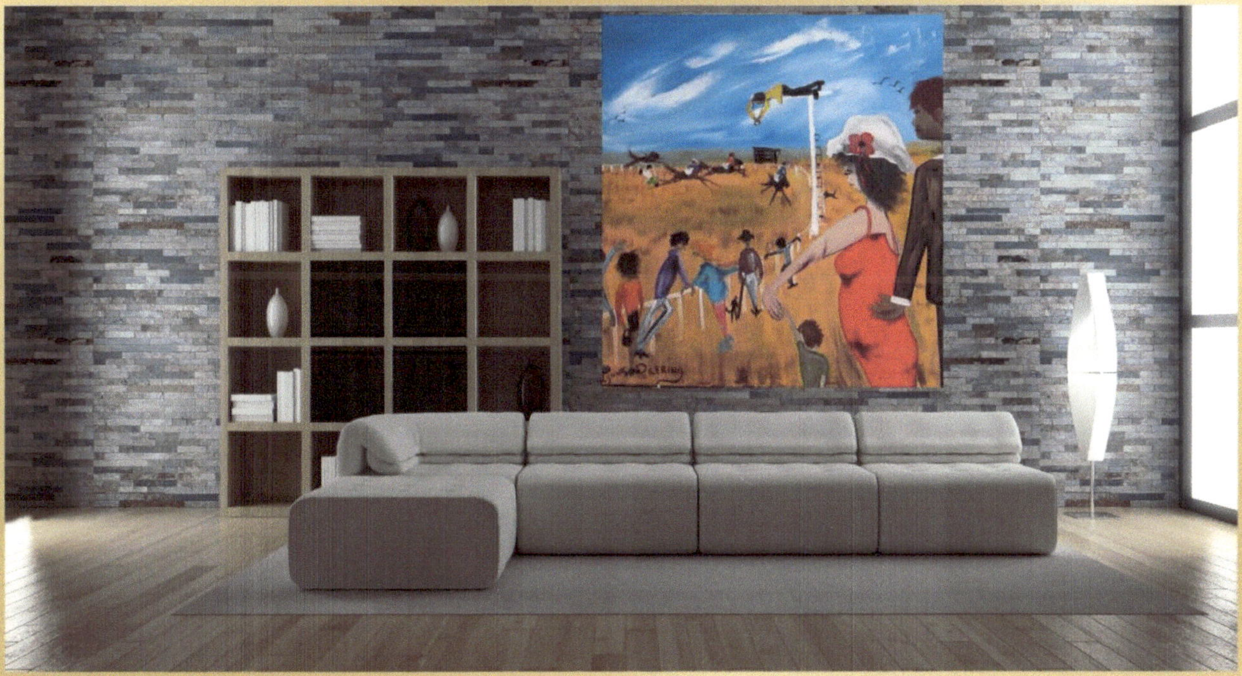

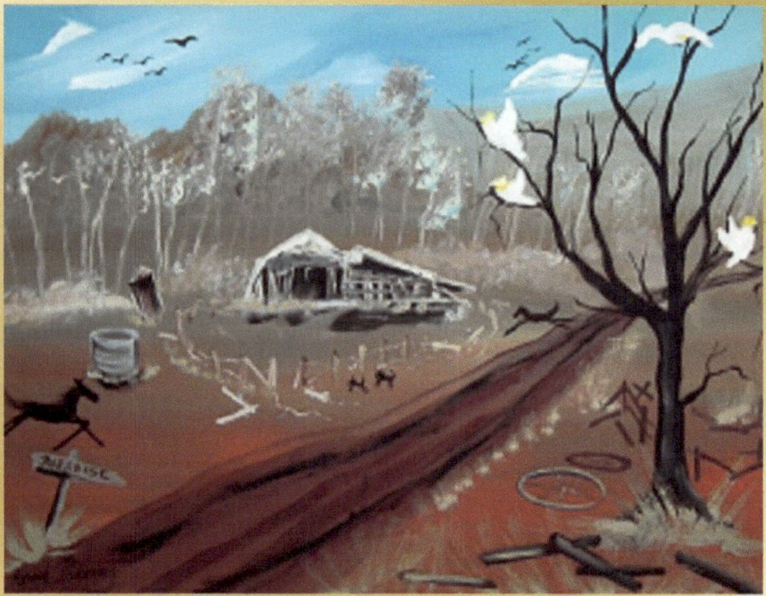

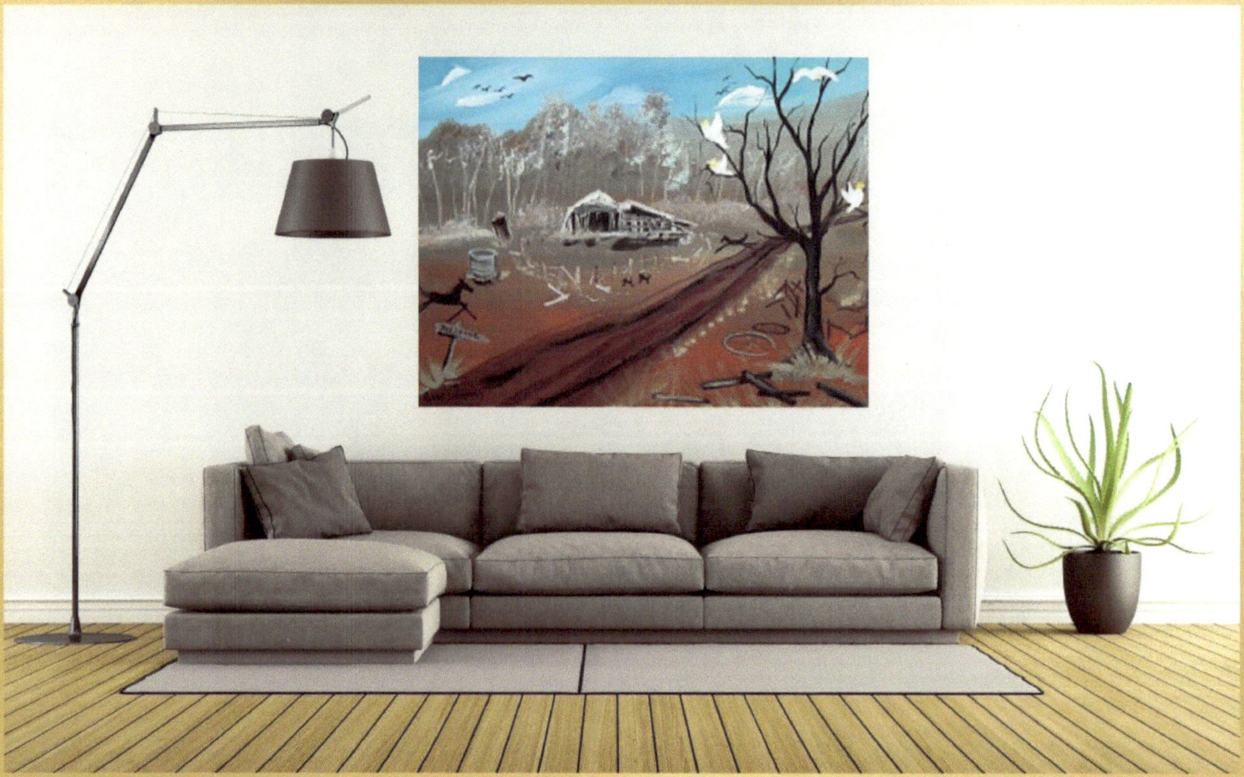

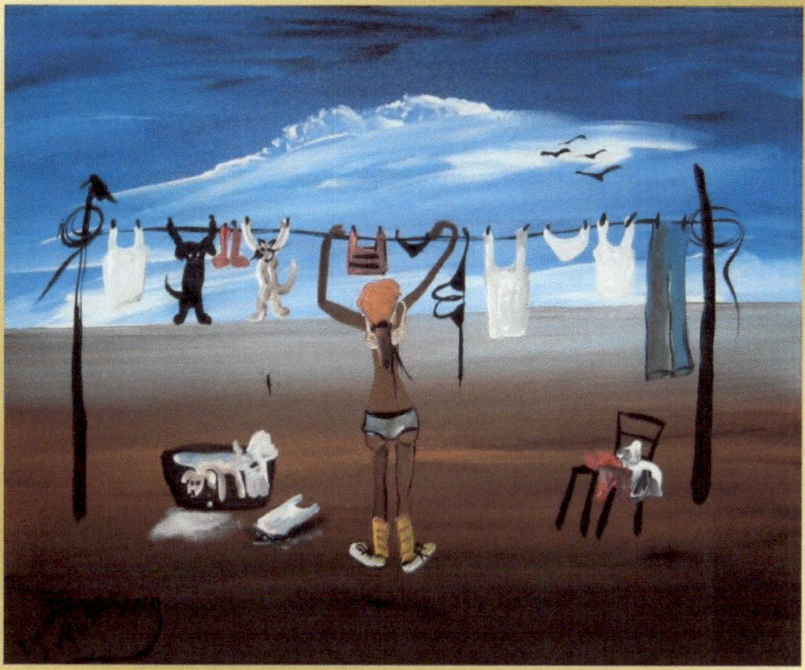

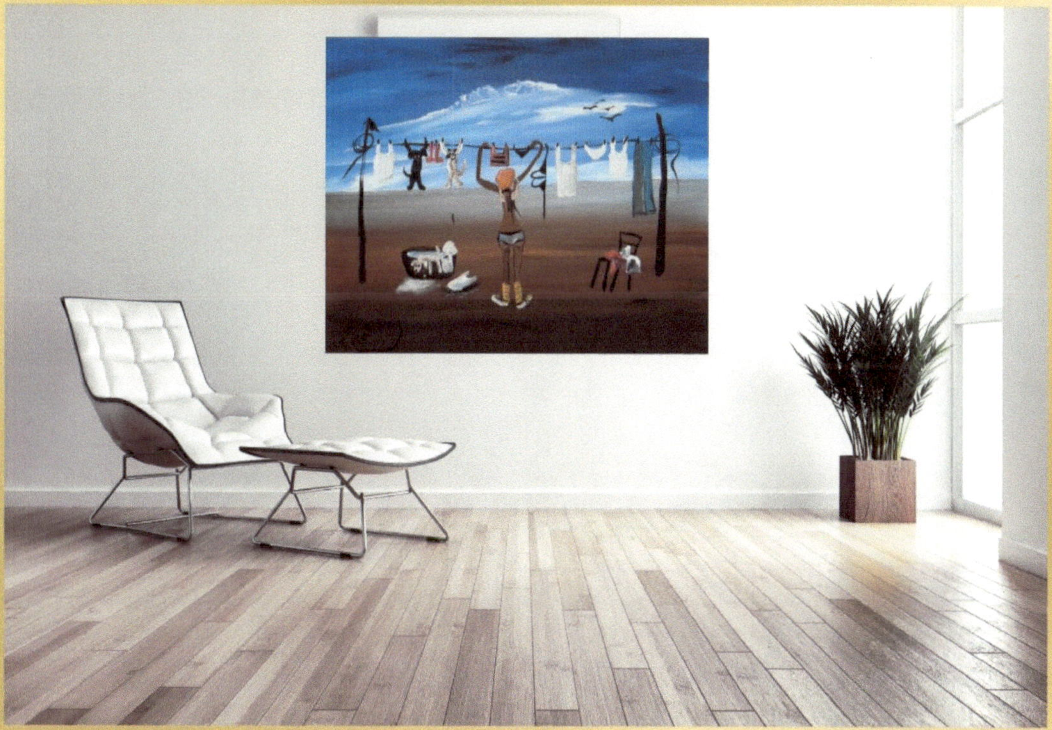

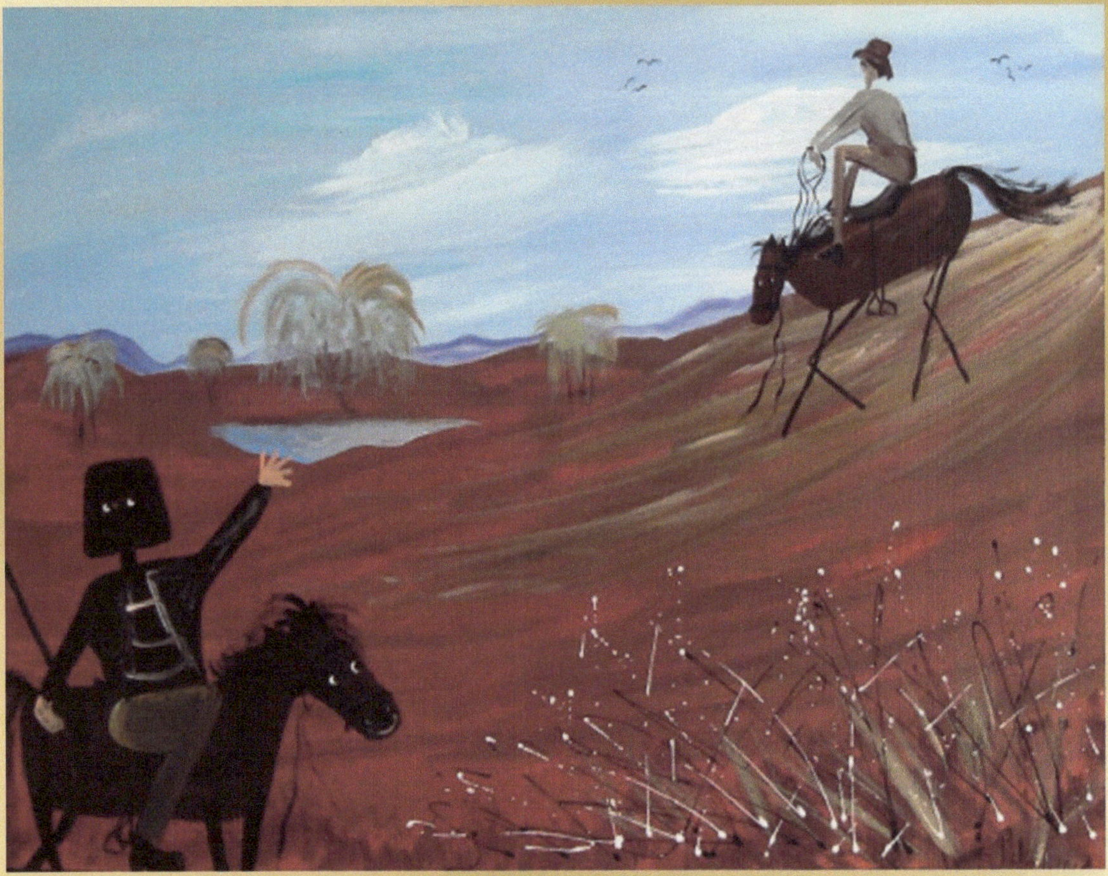

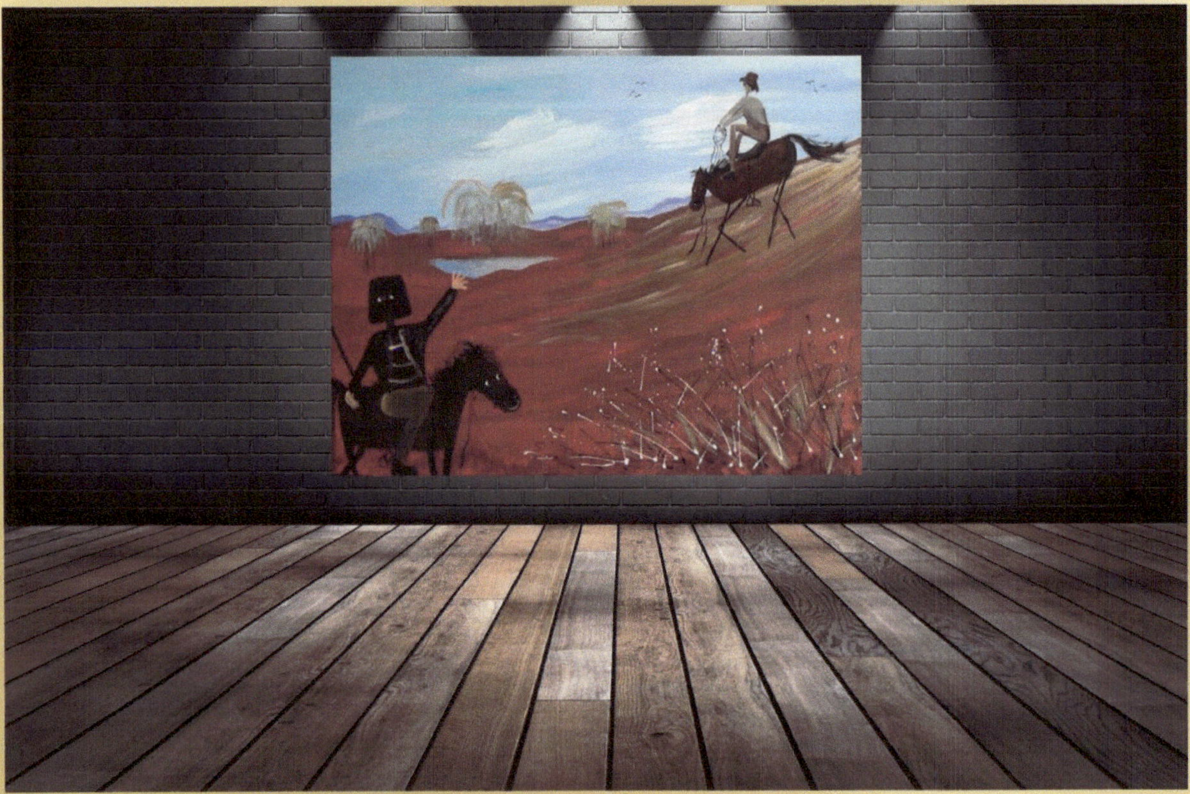

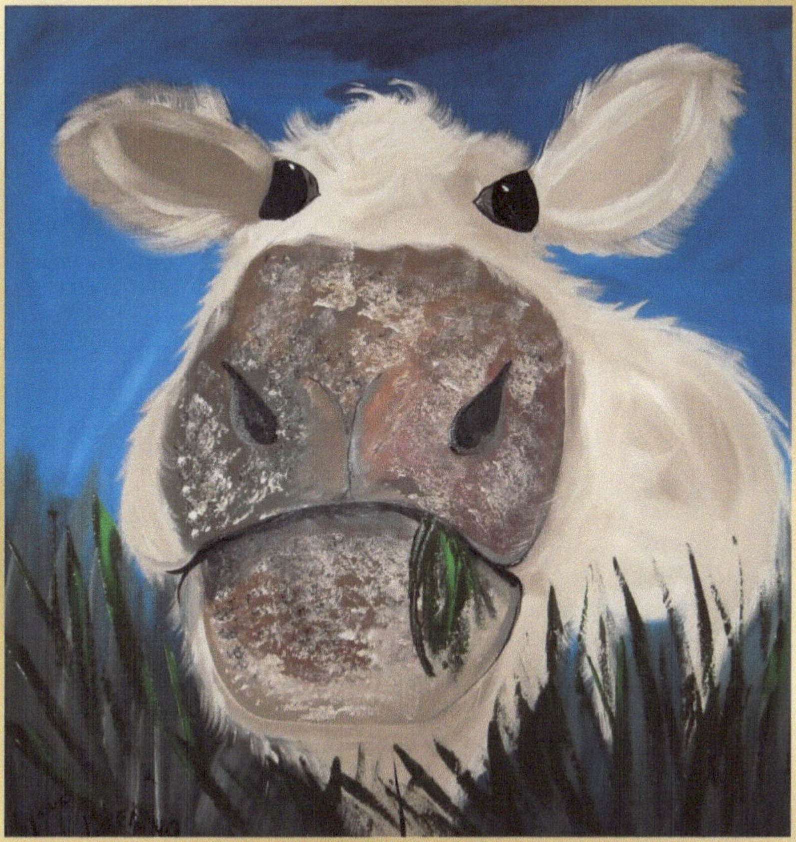

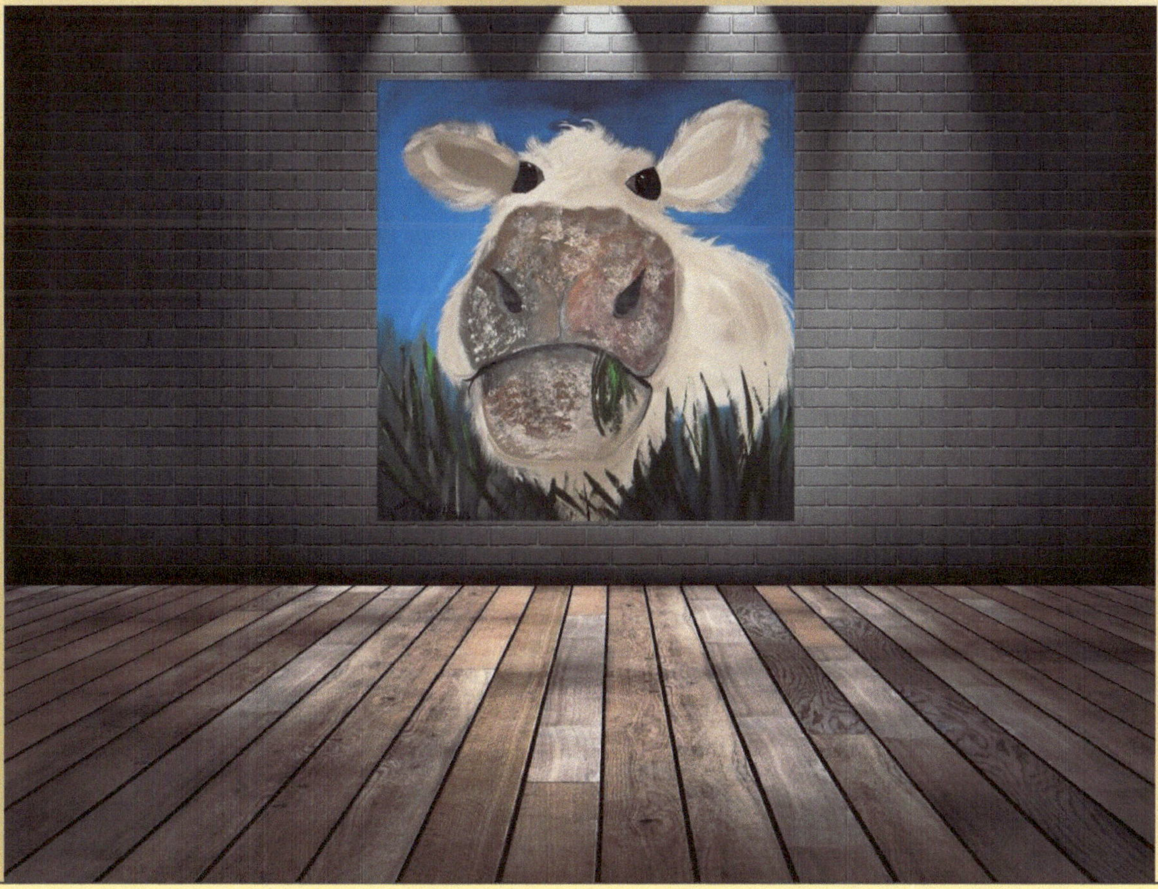

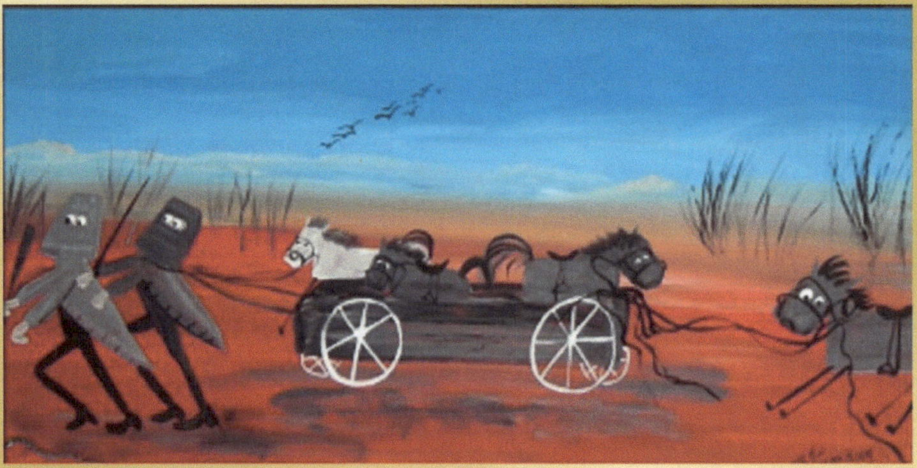

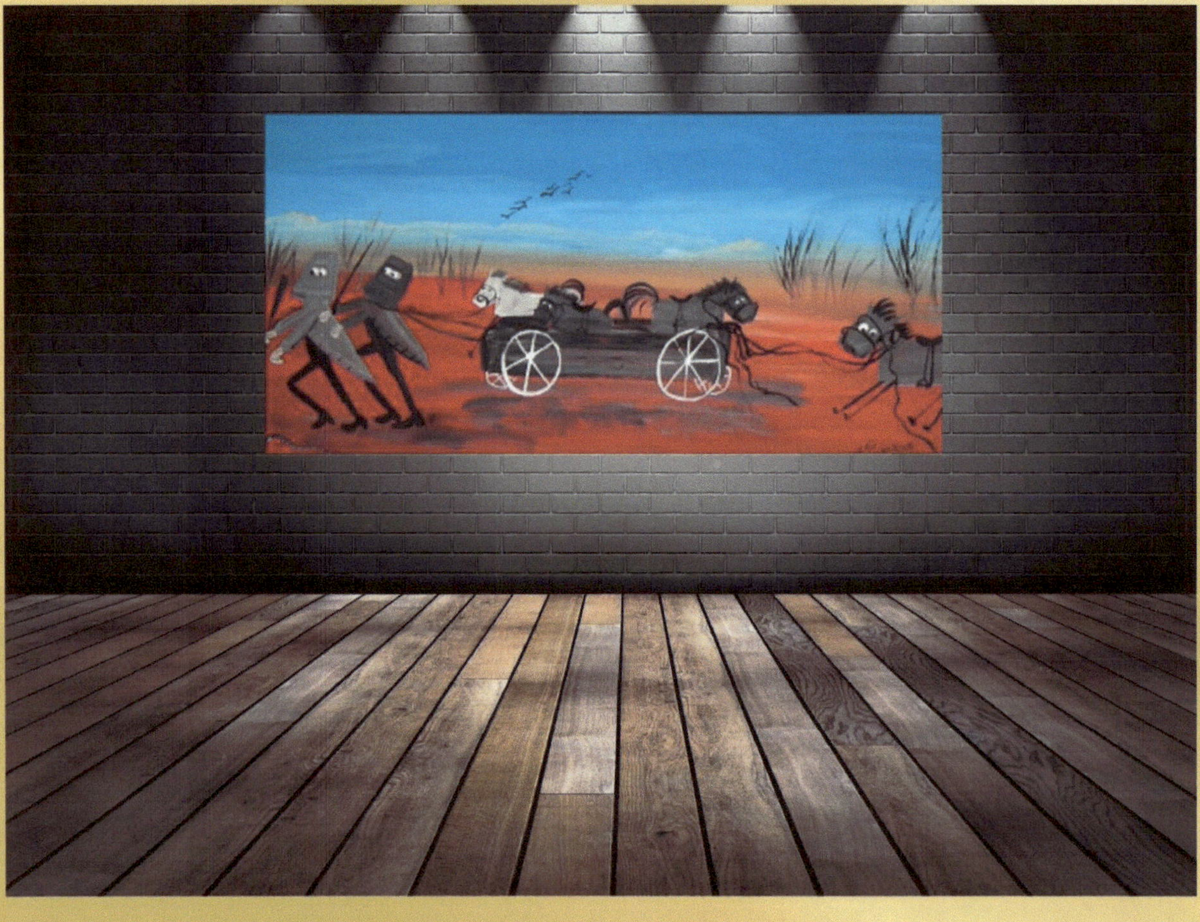

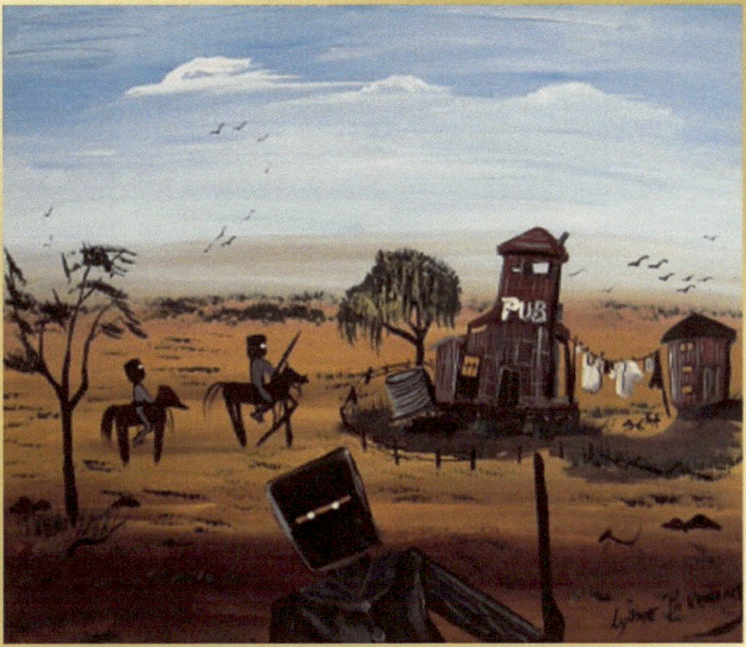
PUB

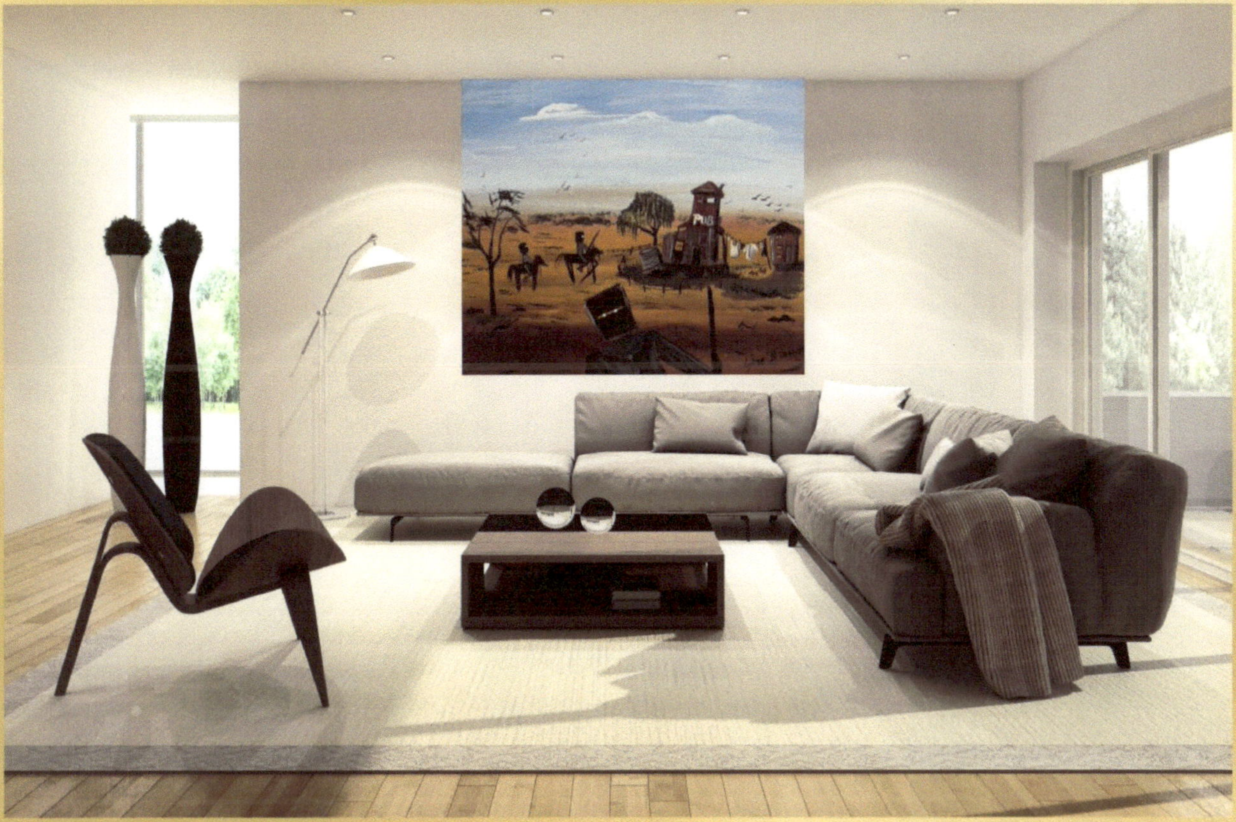

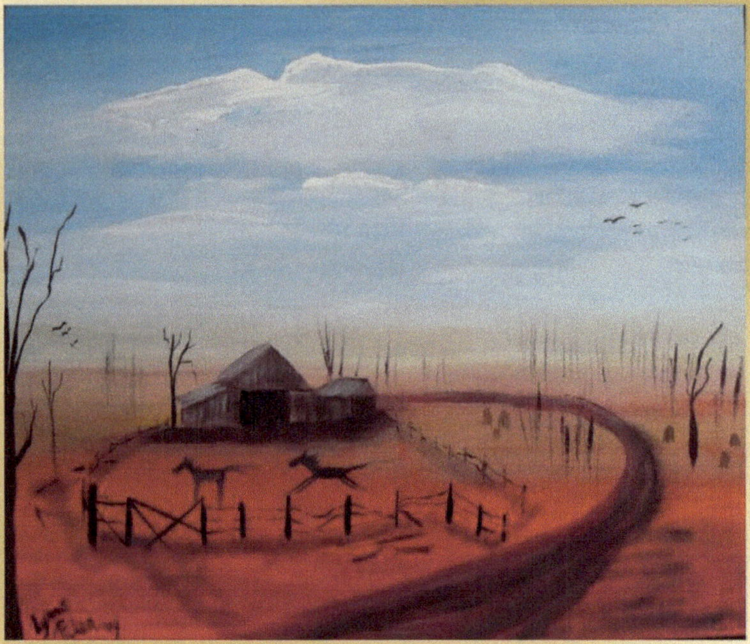

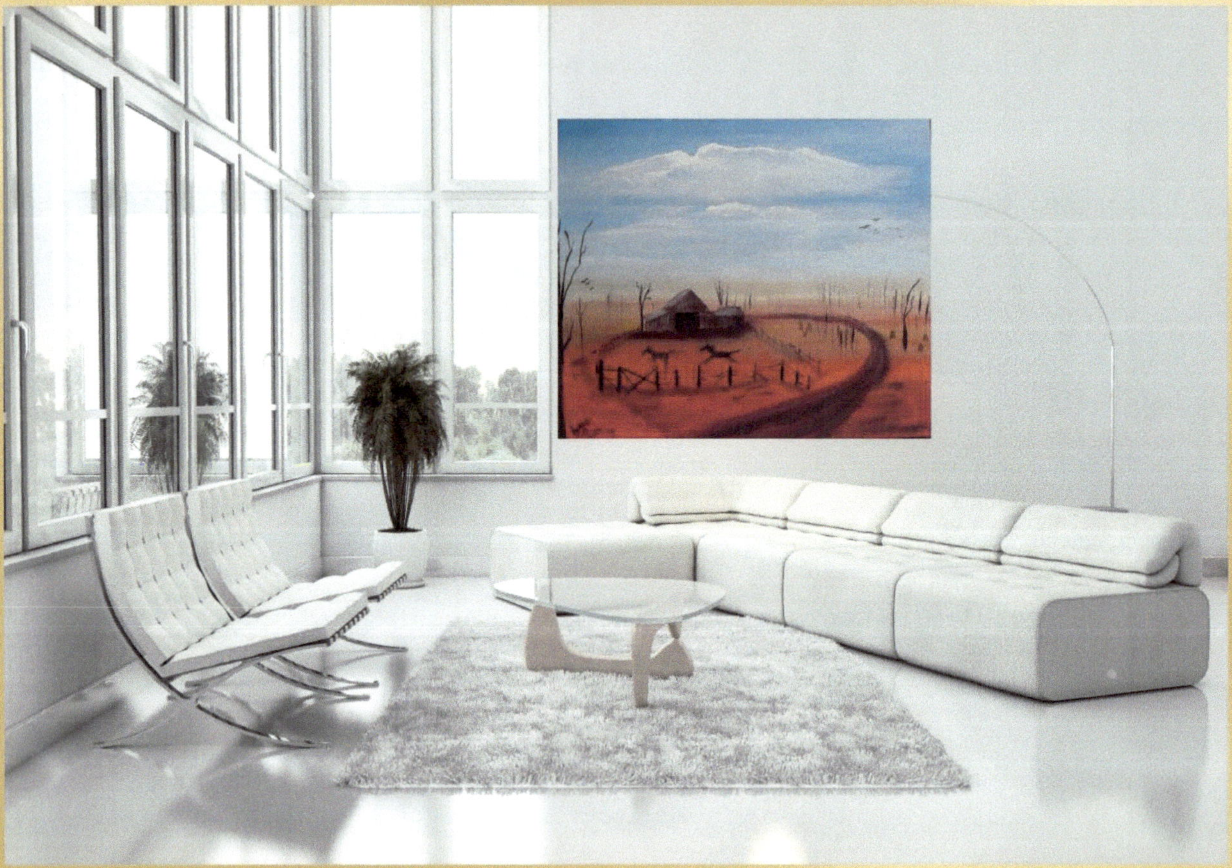

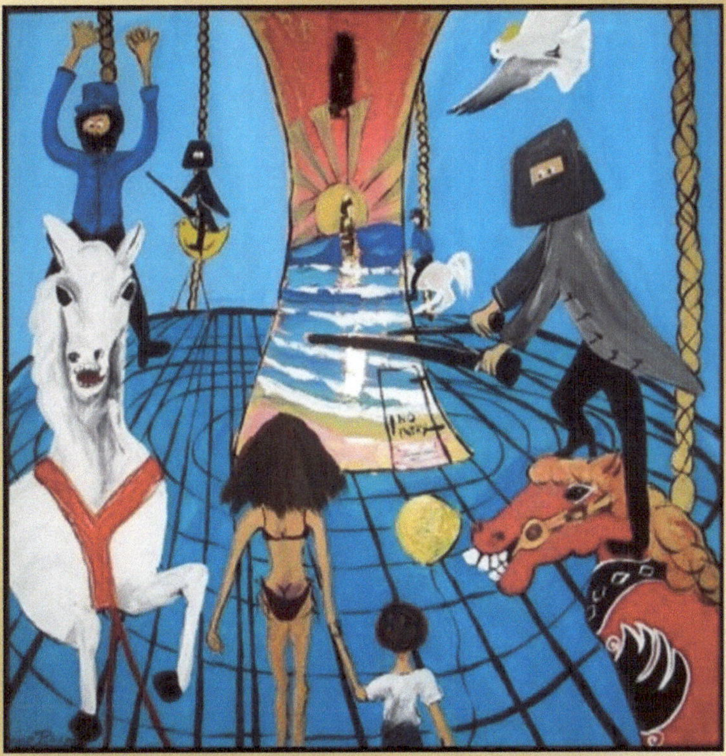

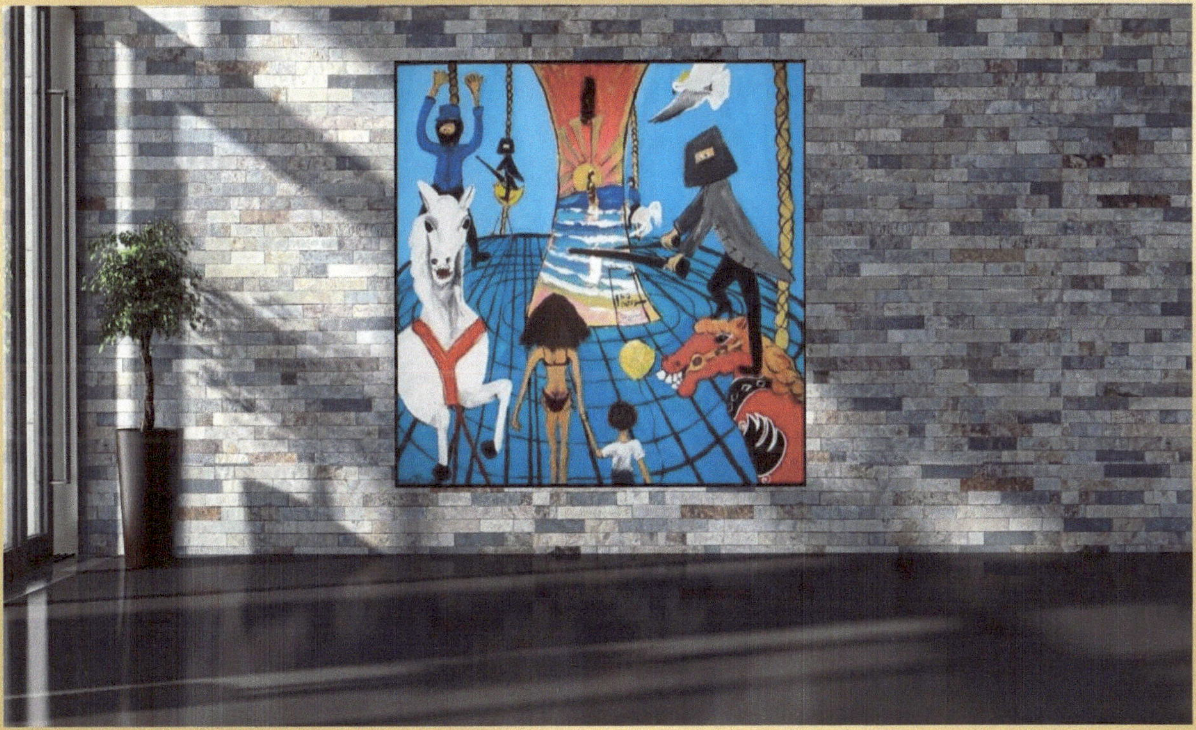

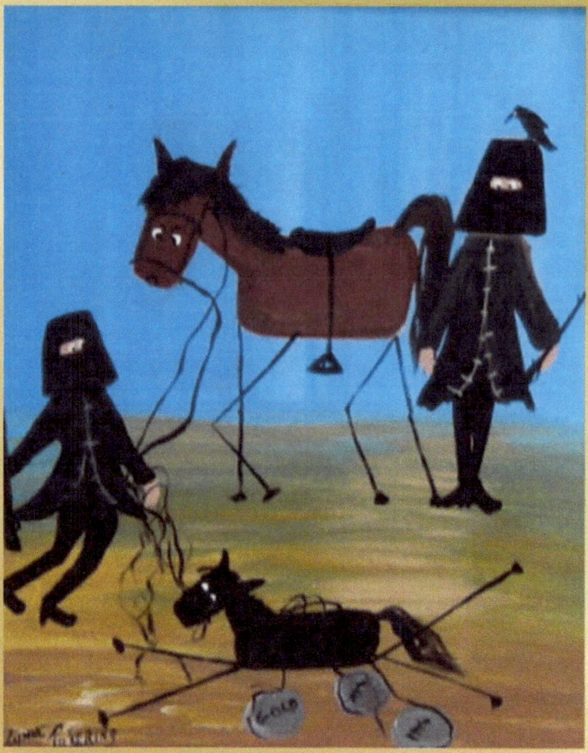
GOLD

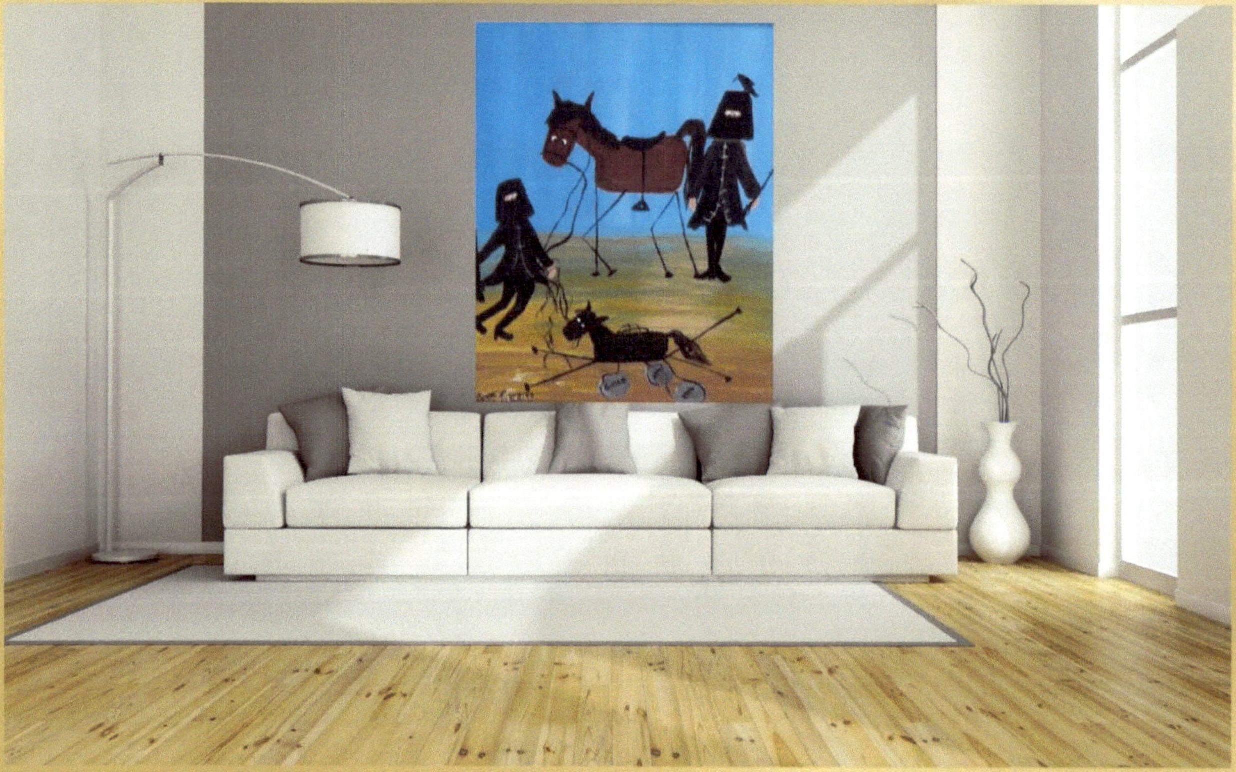

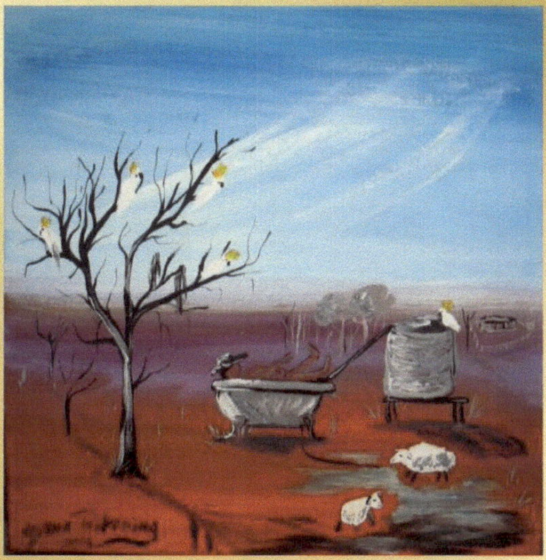

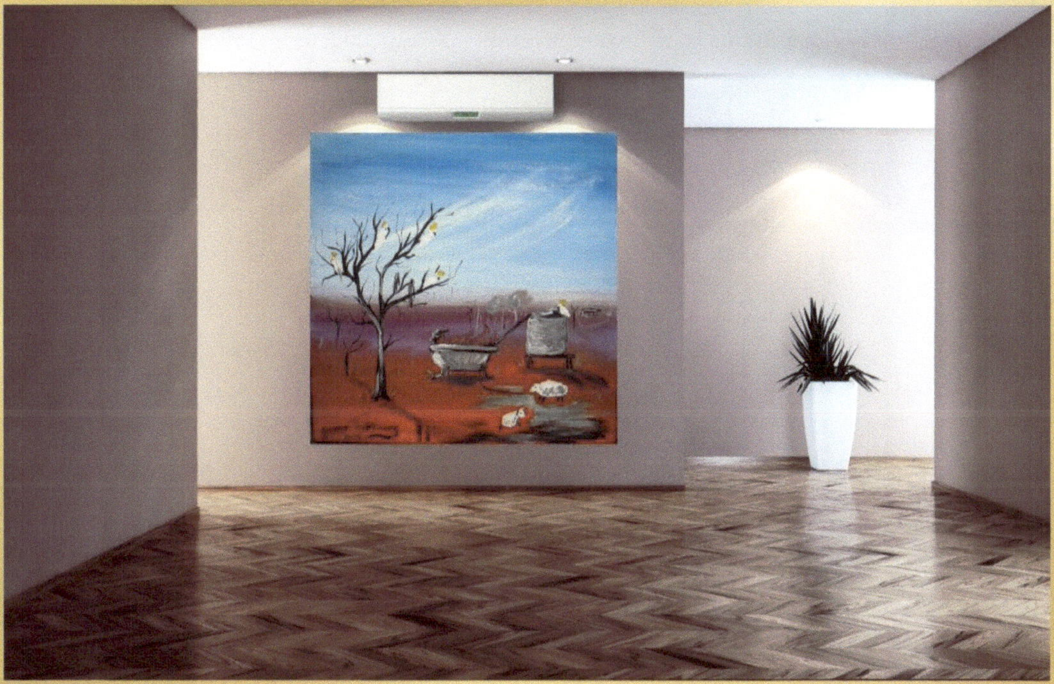

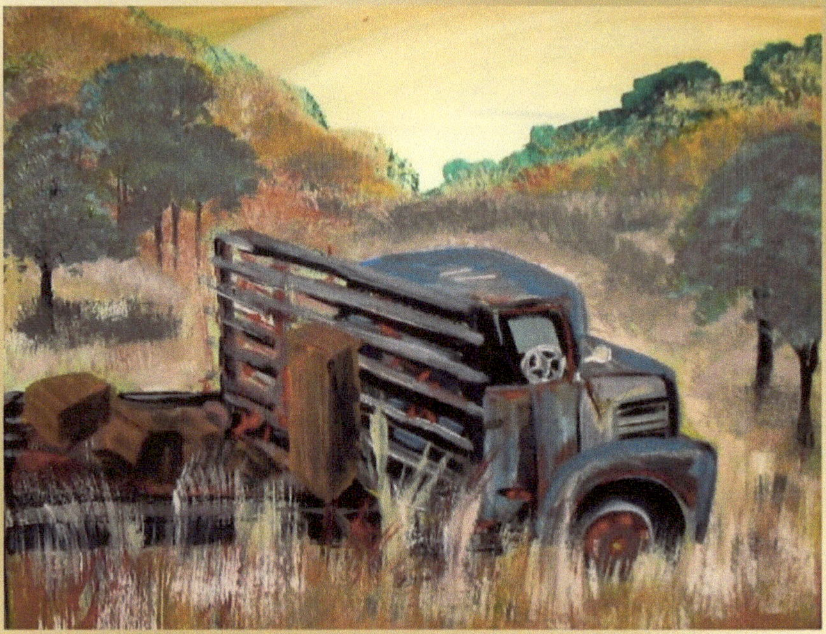

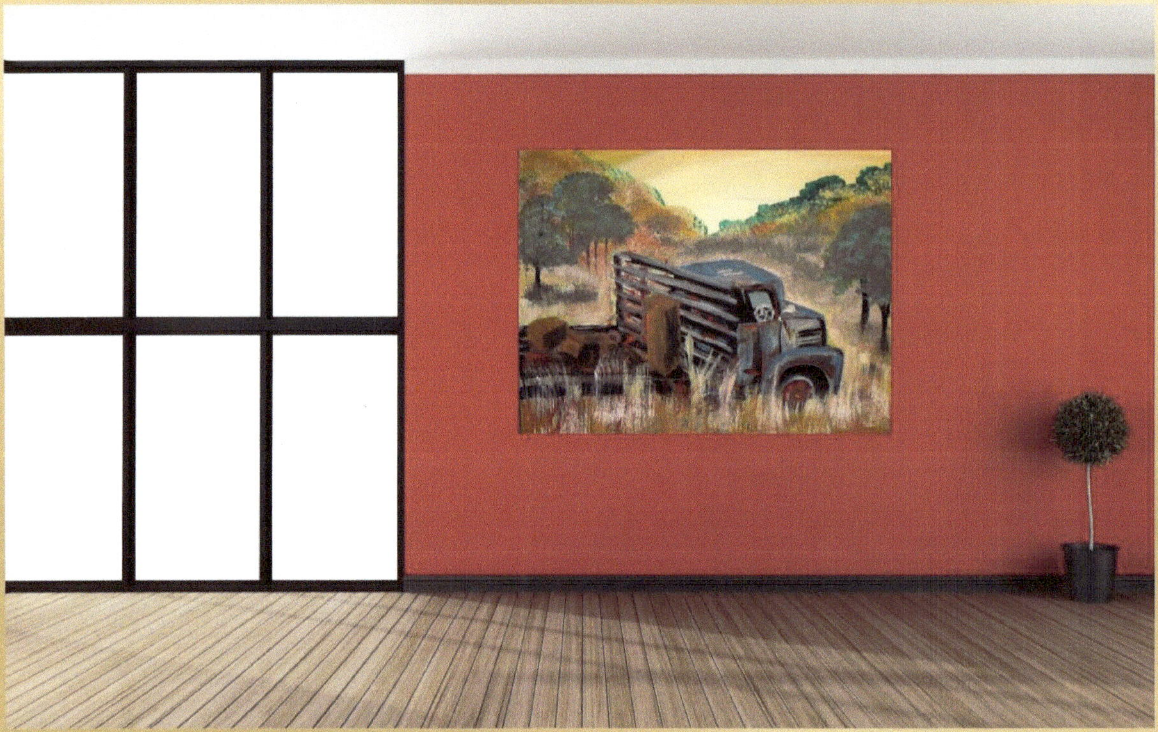

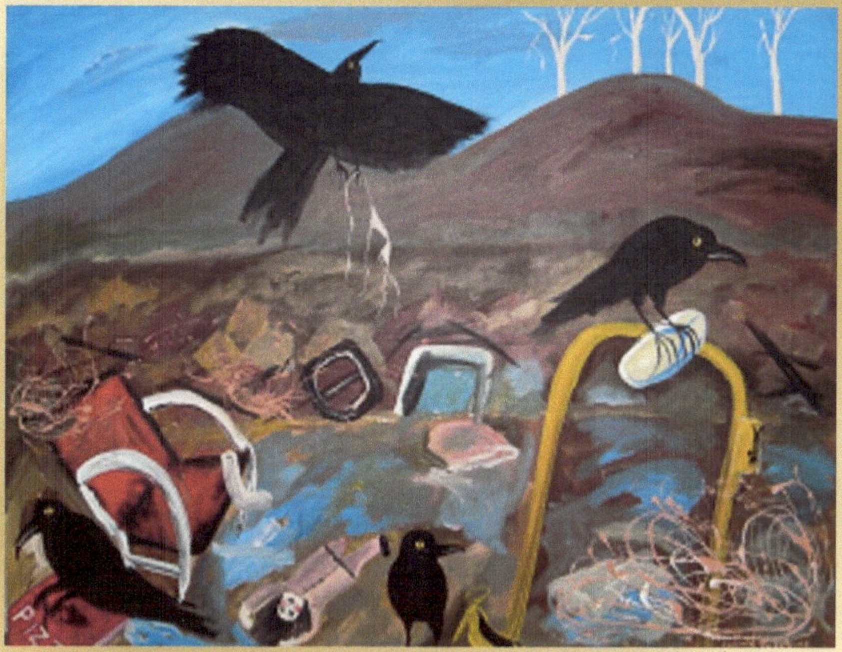

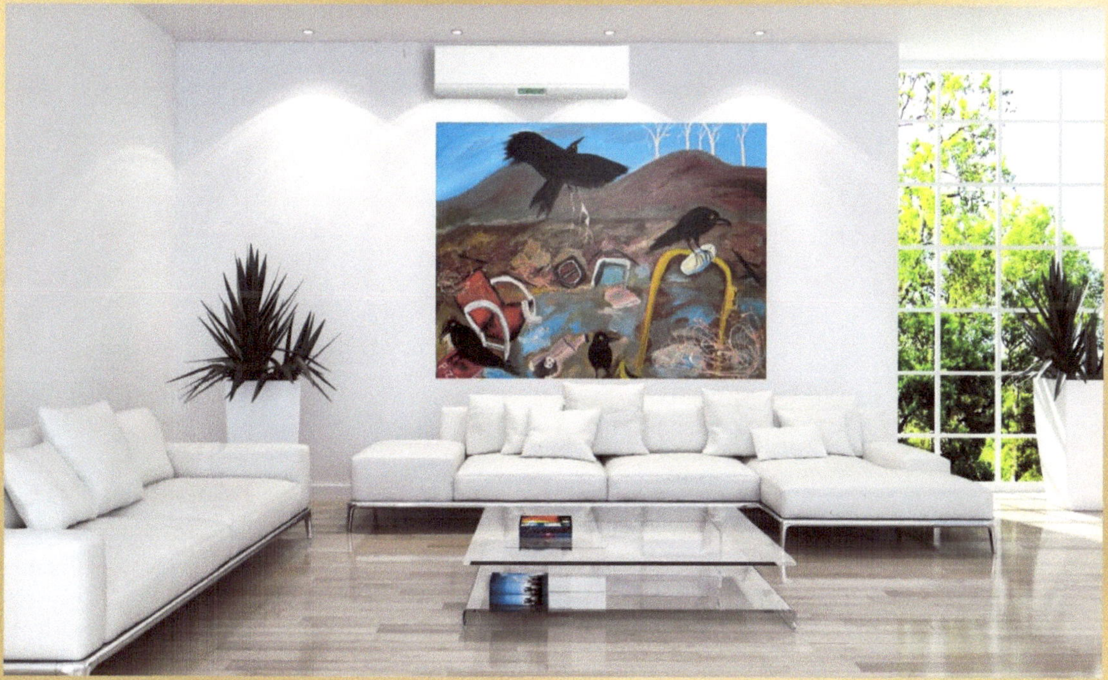

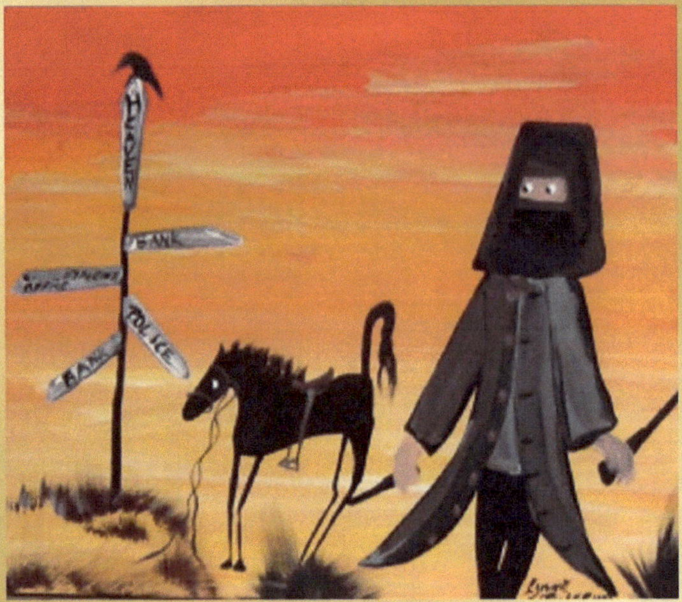
BANK
POLICE
BANK

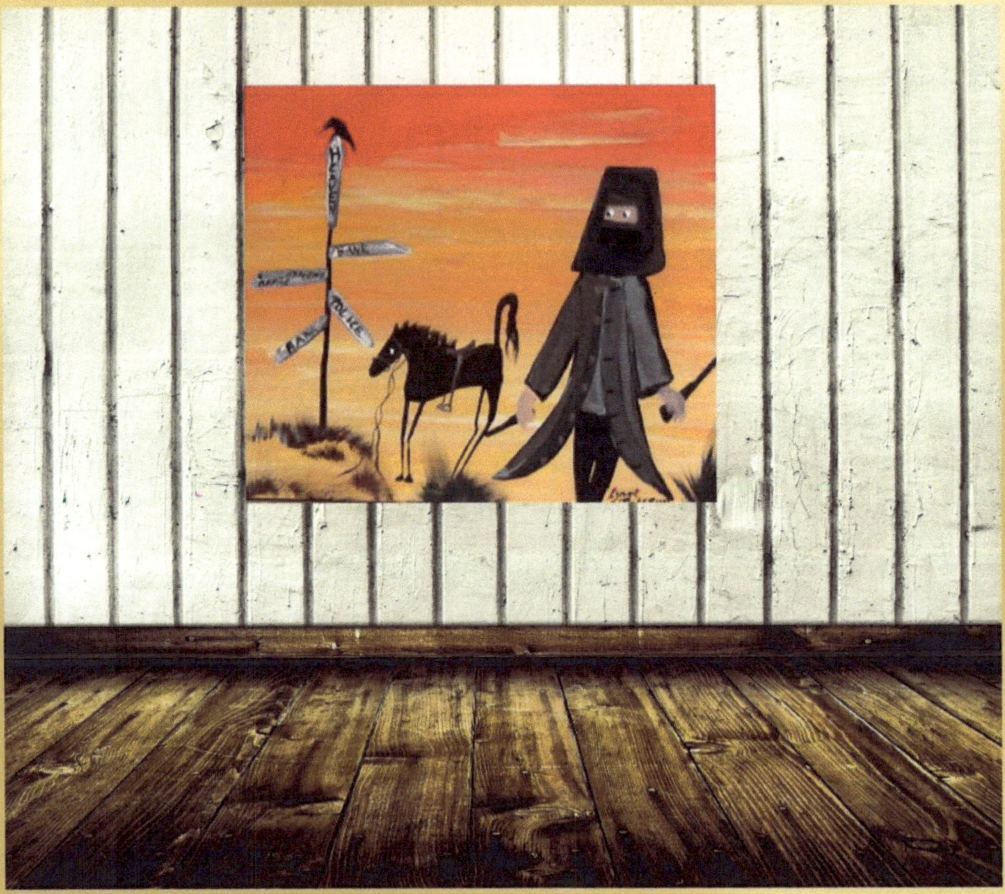

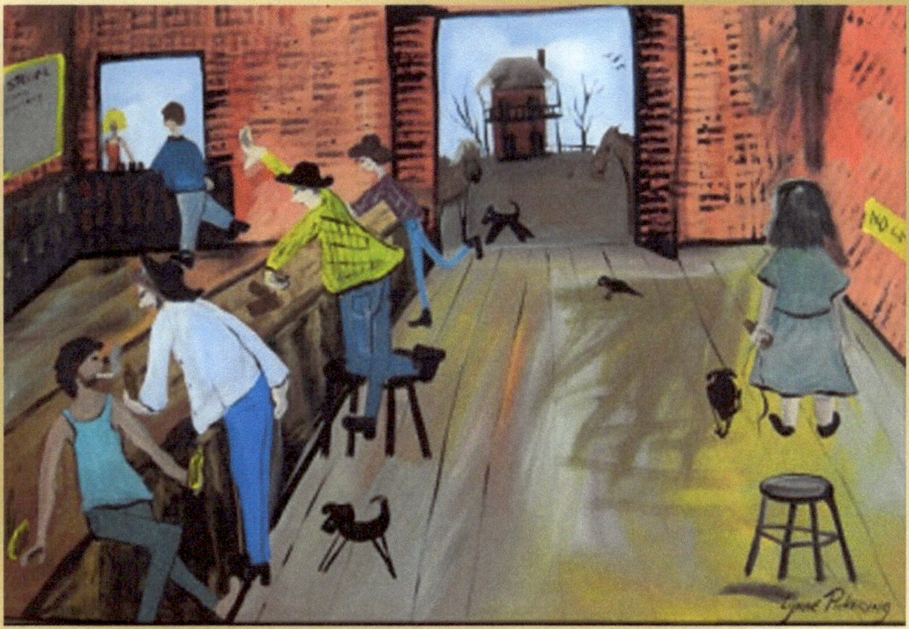

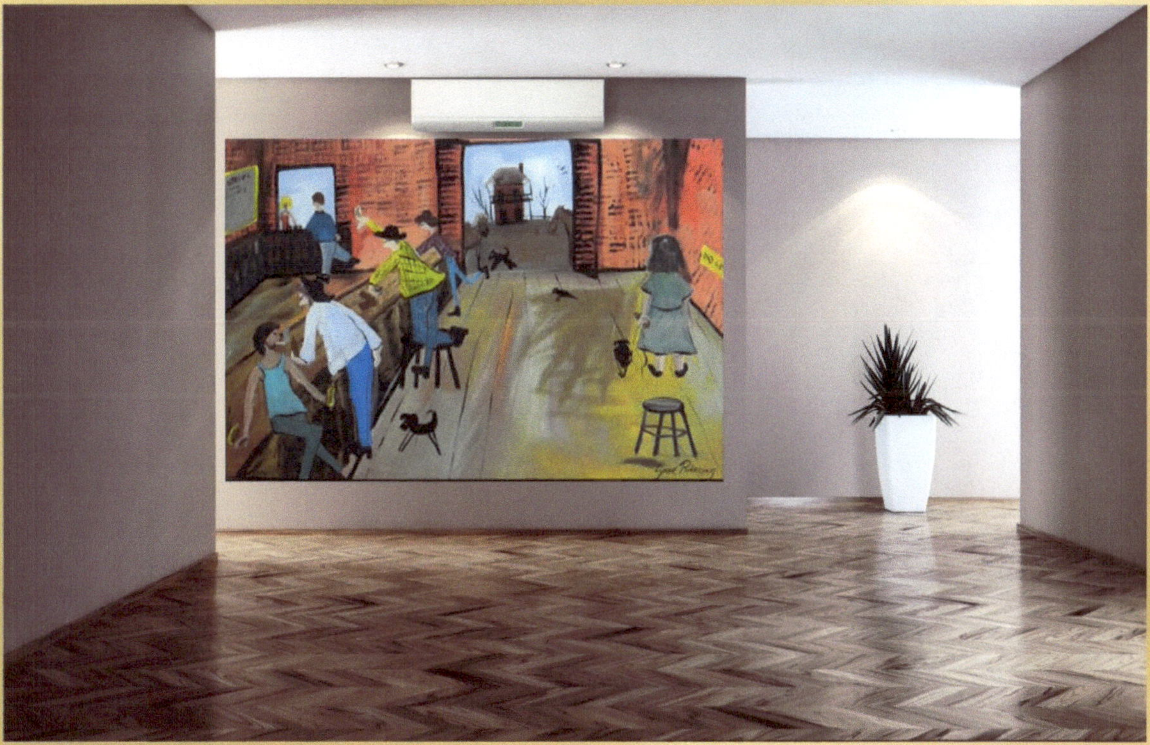

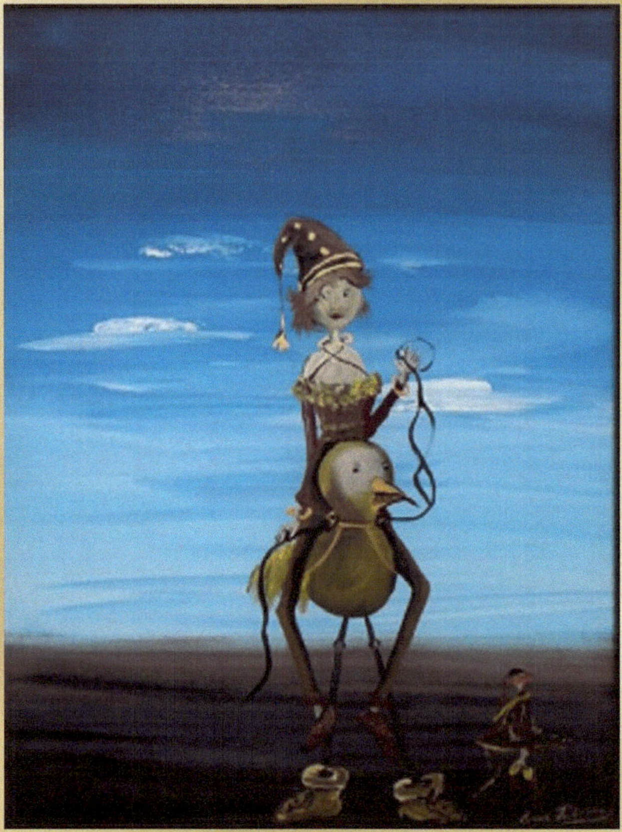

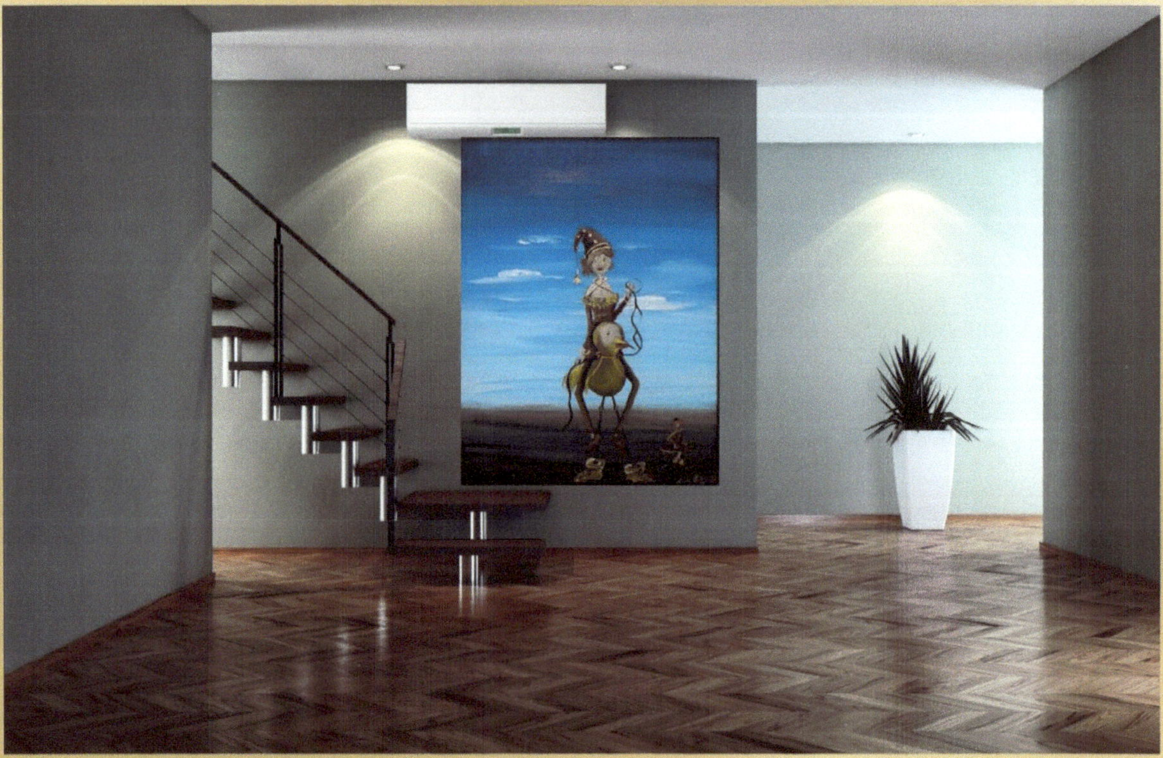

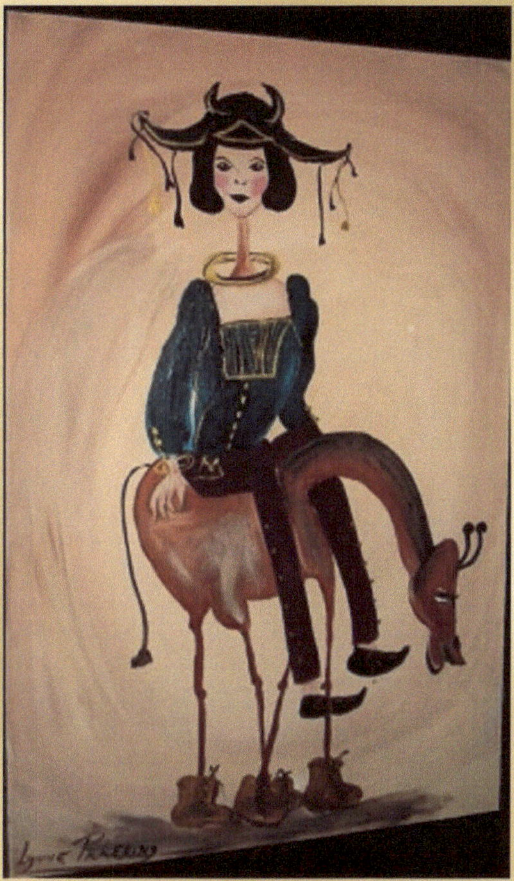

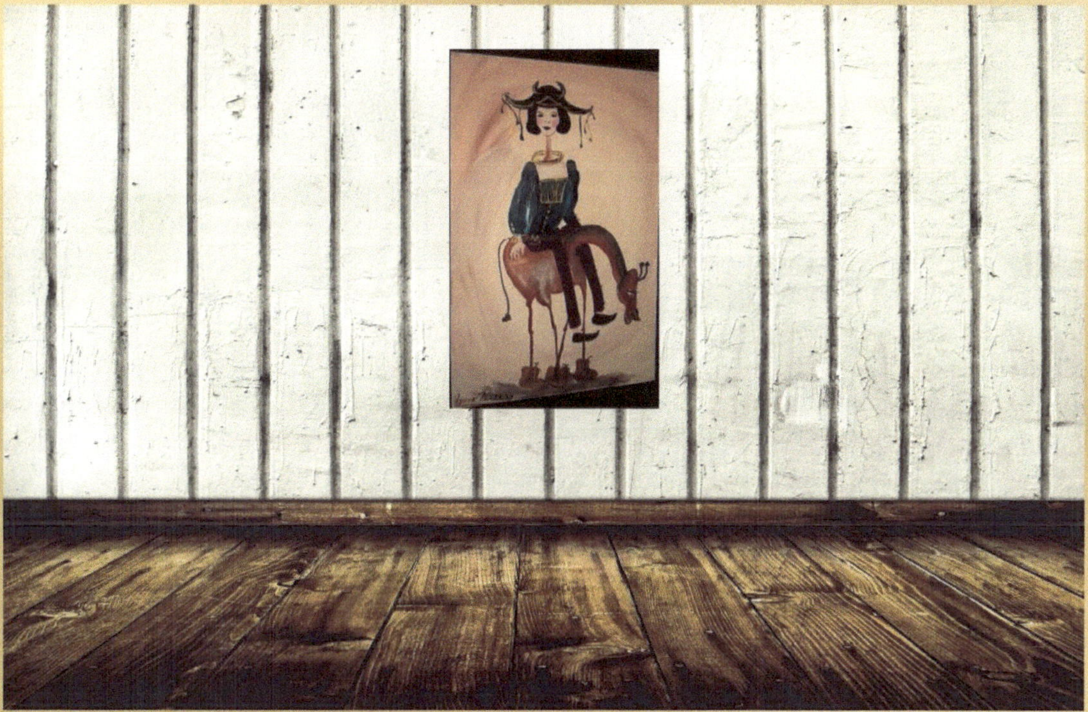

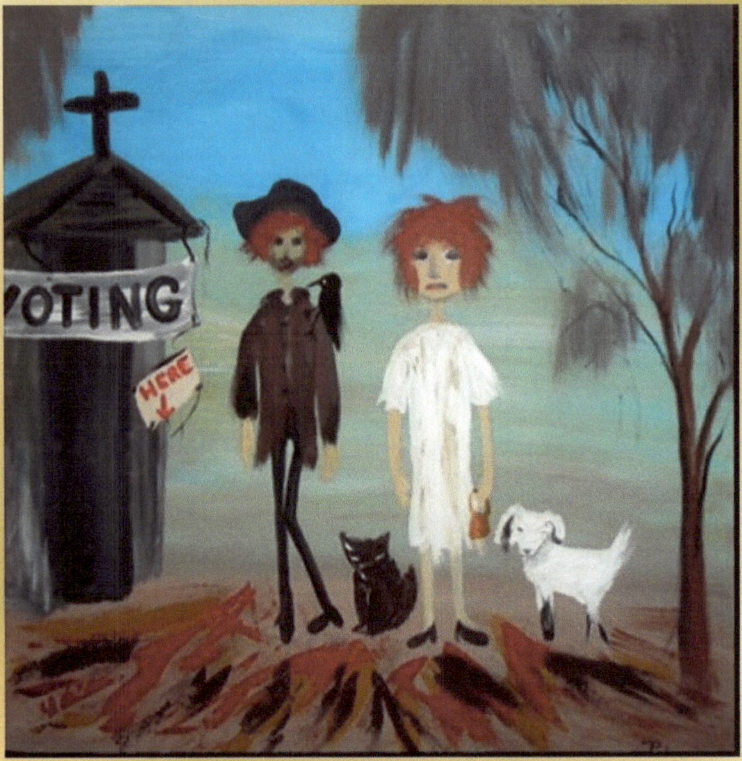
VOTING
HERE

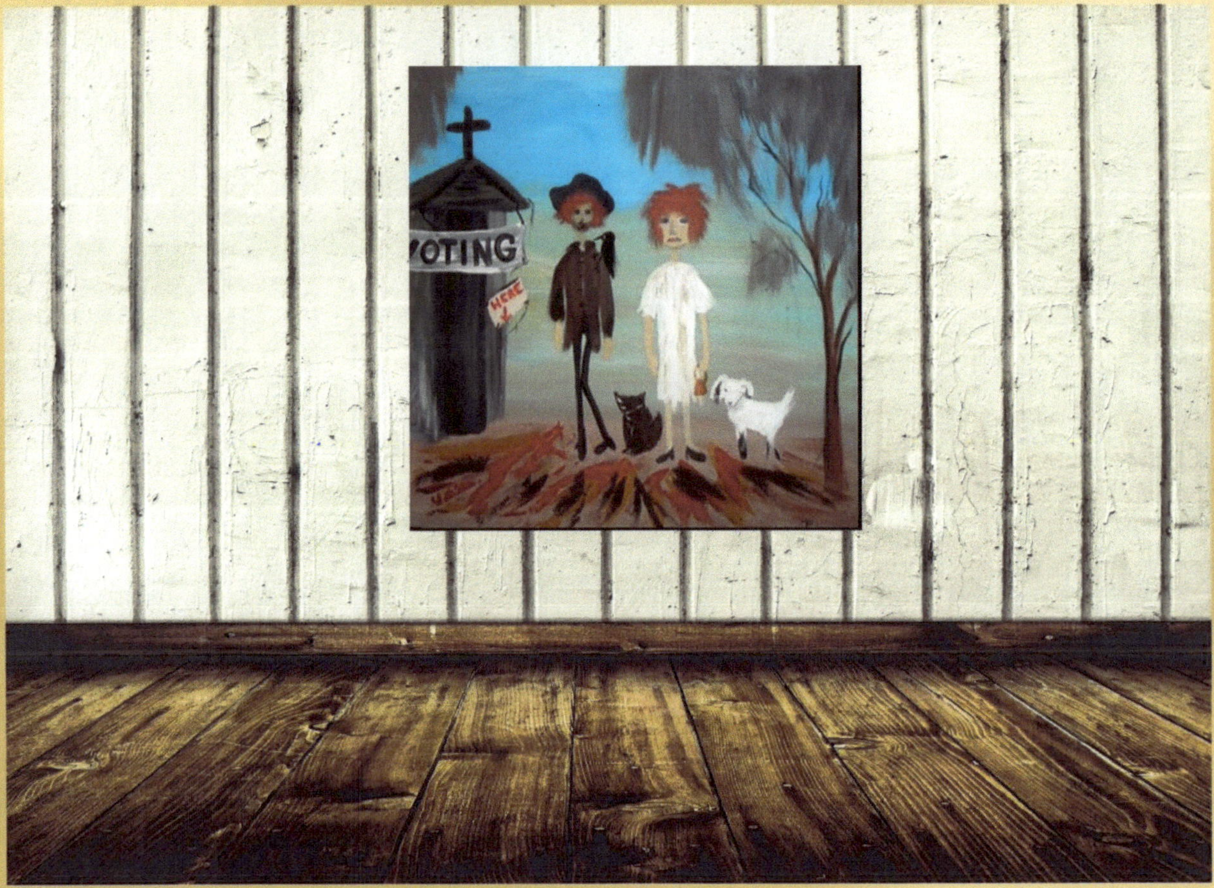
VOTING
HERE

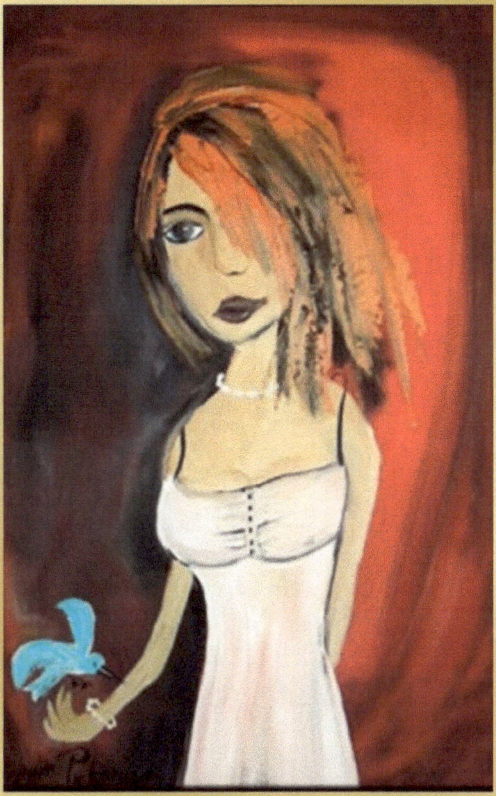

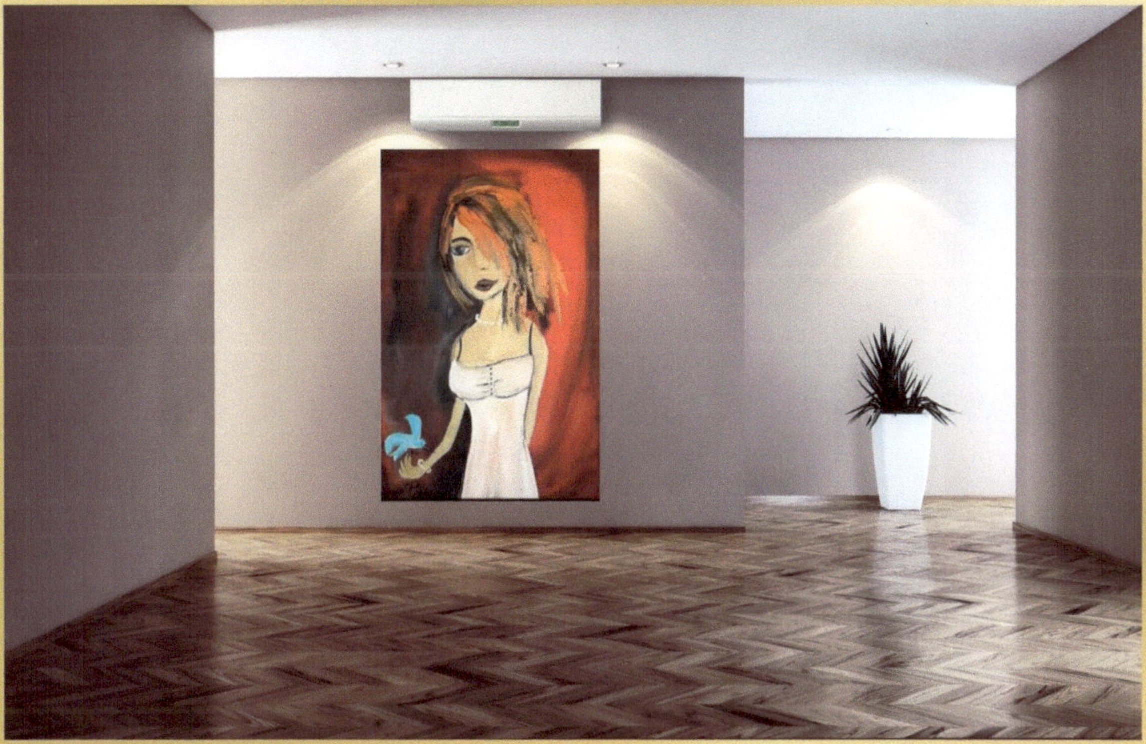

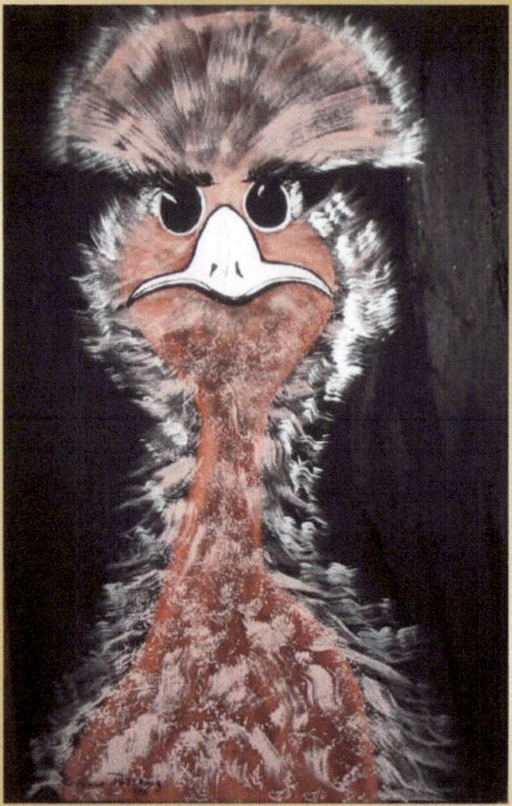

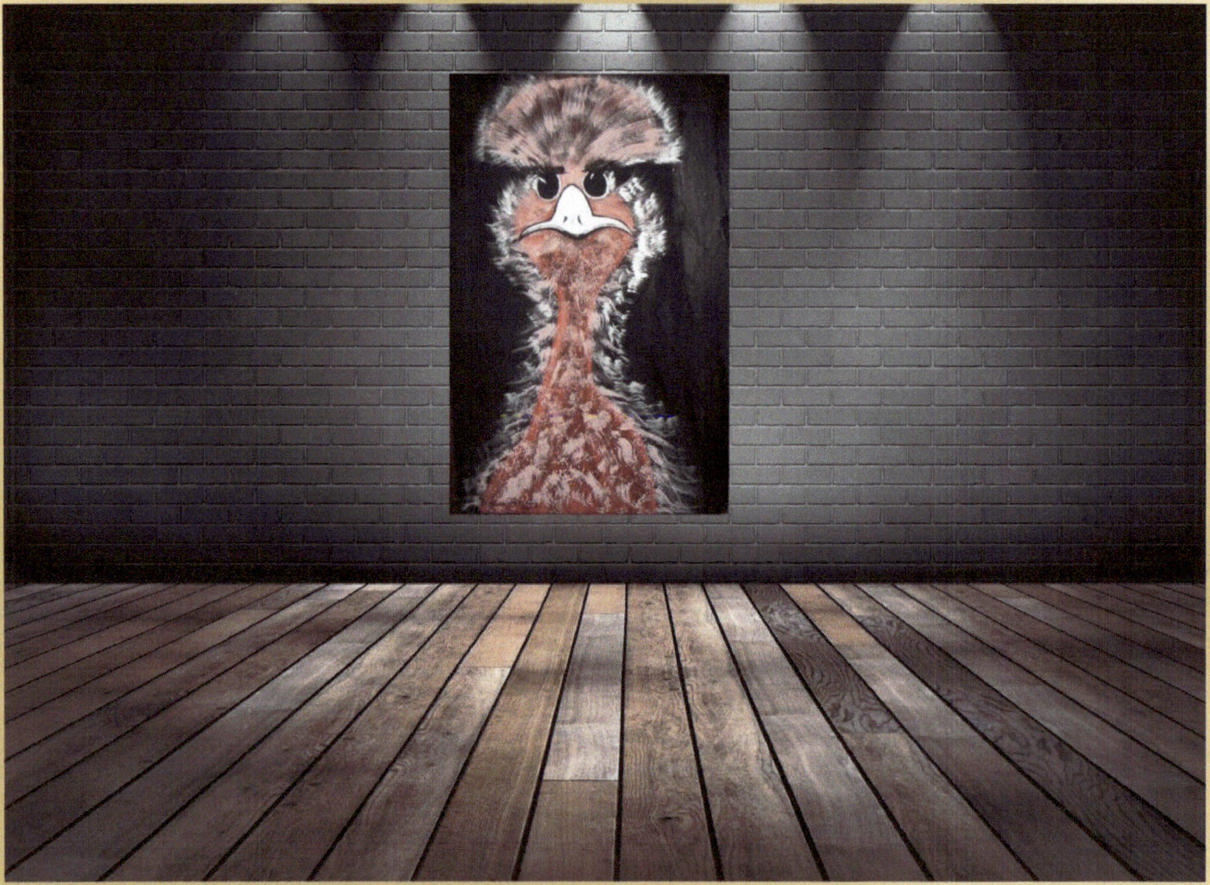

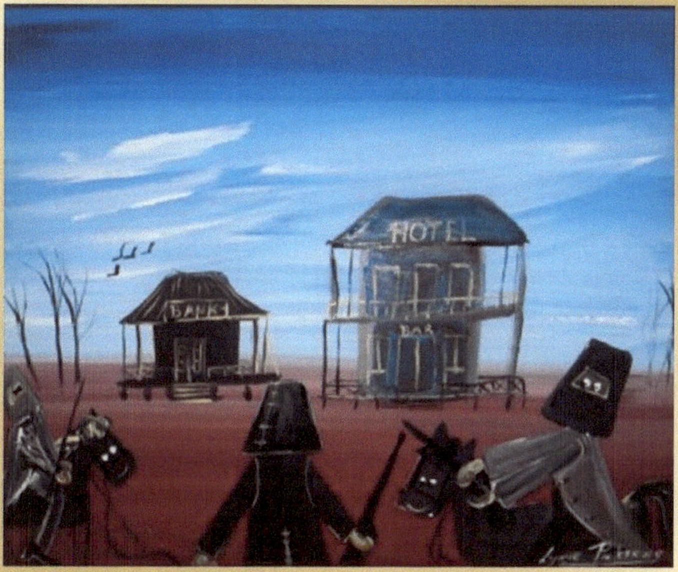
BANK
HOTEL
BAR

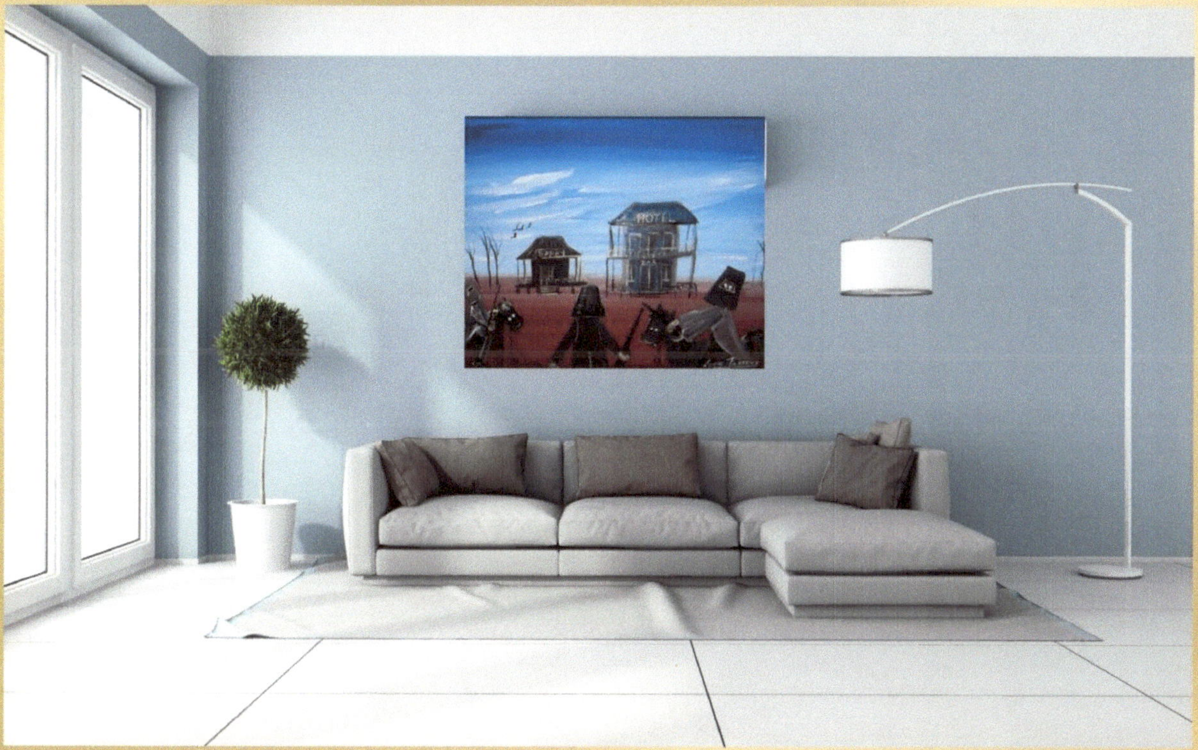

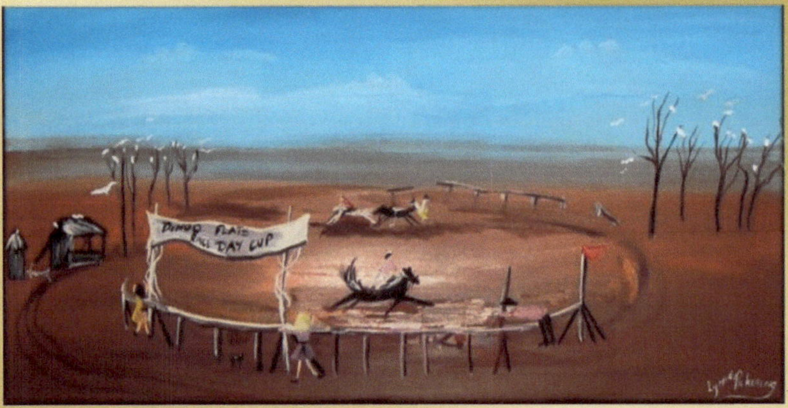

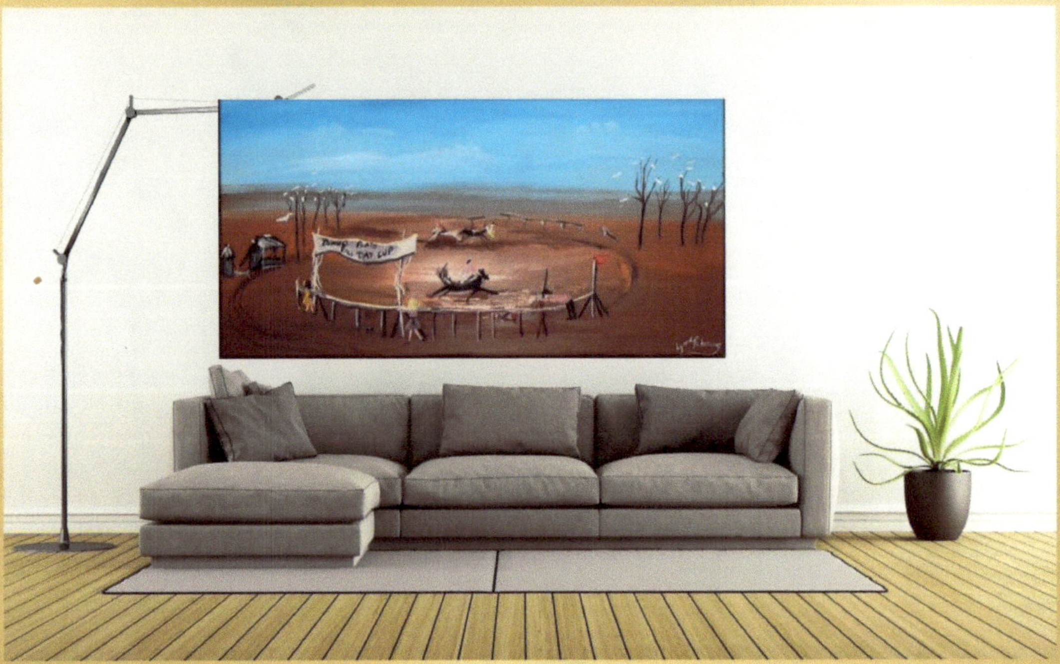

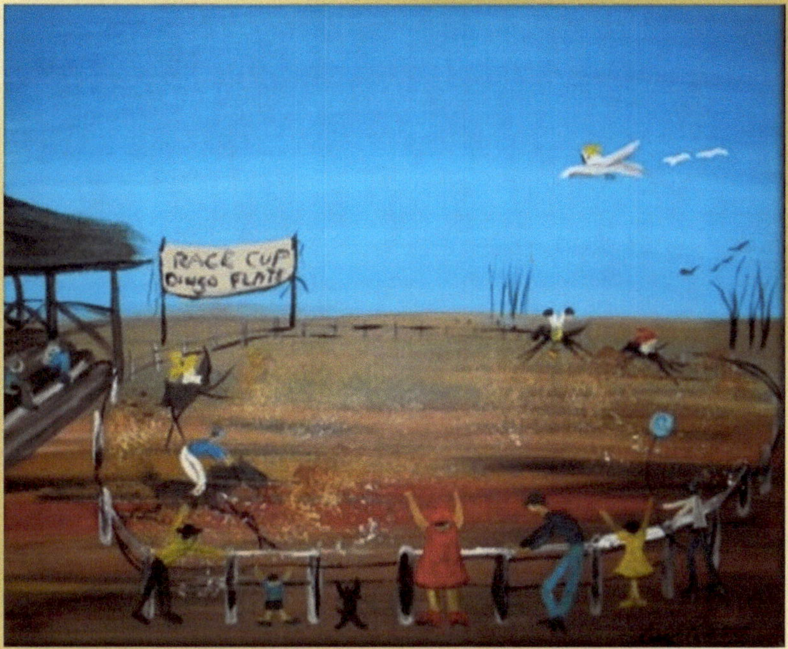
RACE CUP
DINGO FLATS

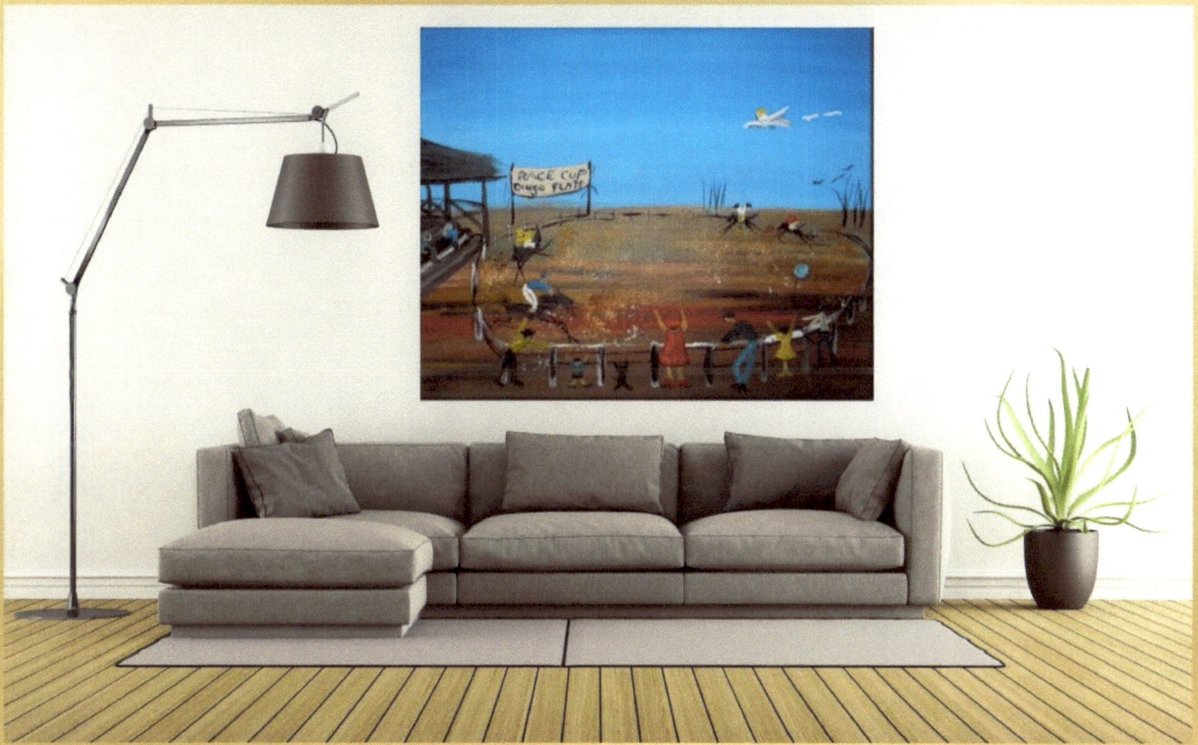

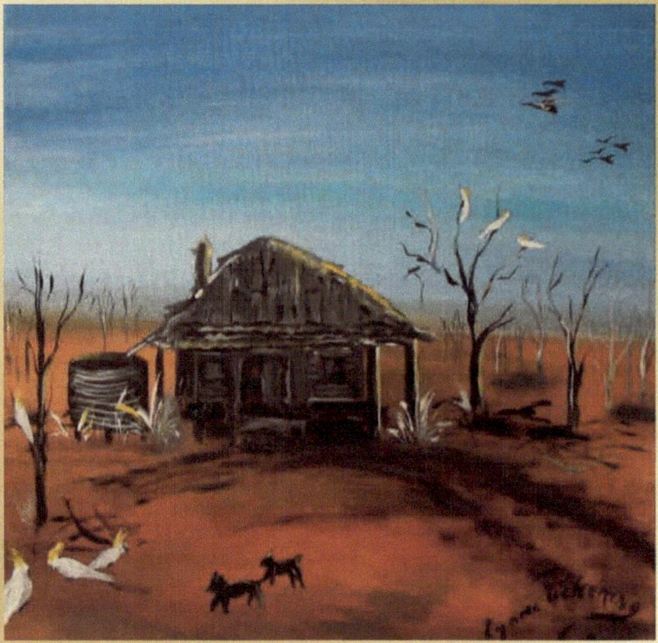

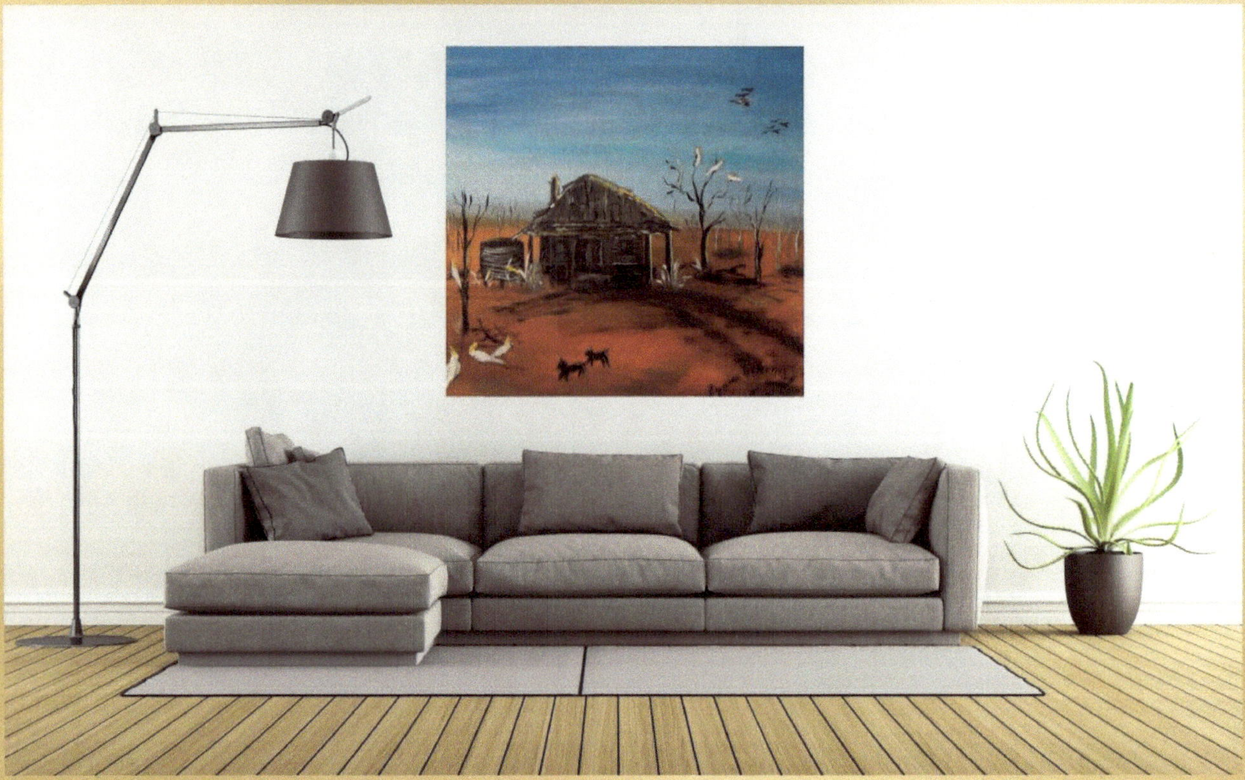

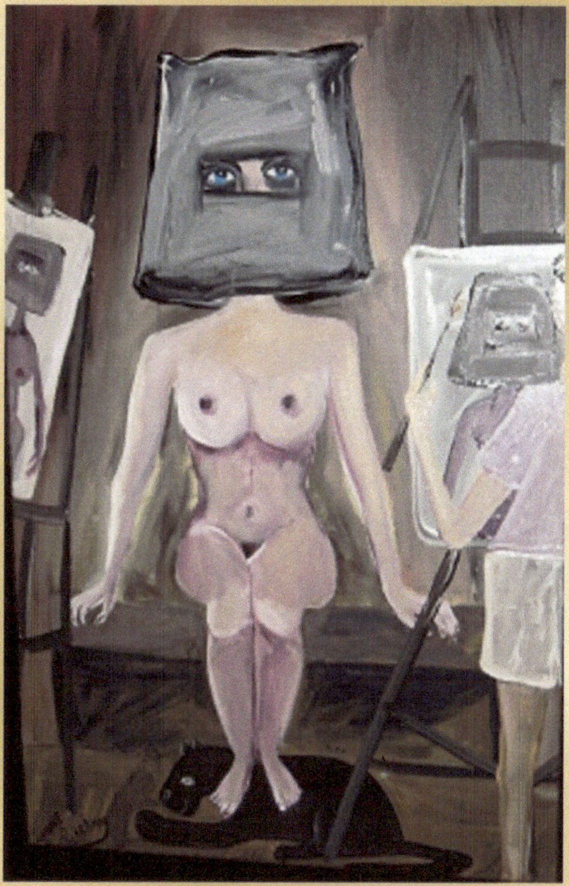

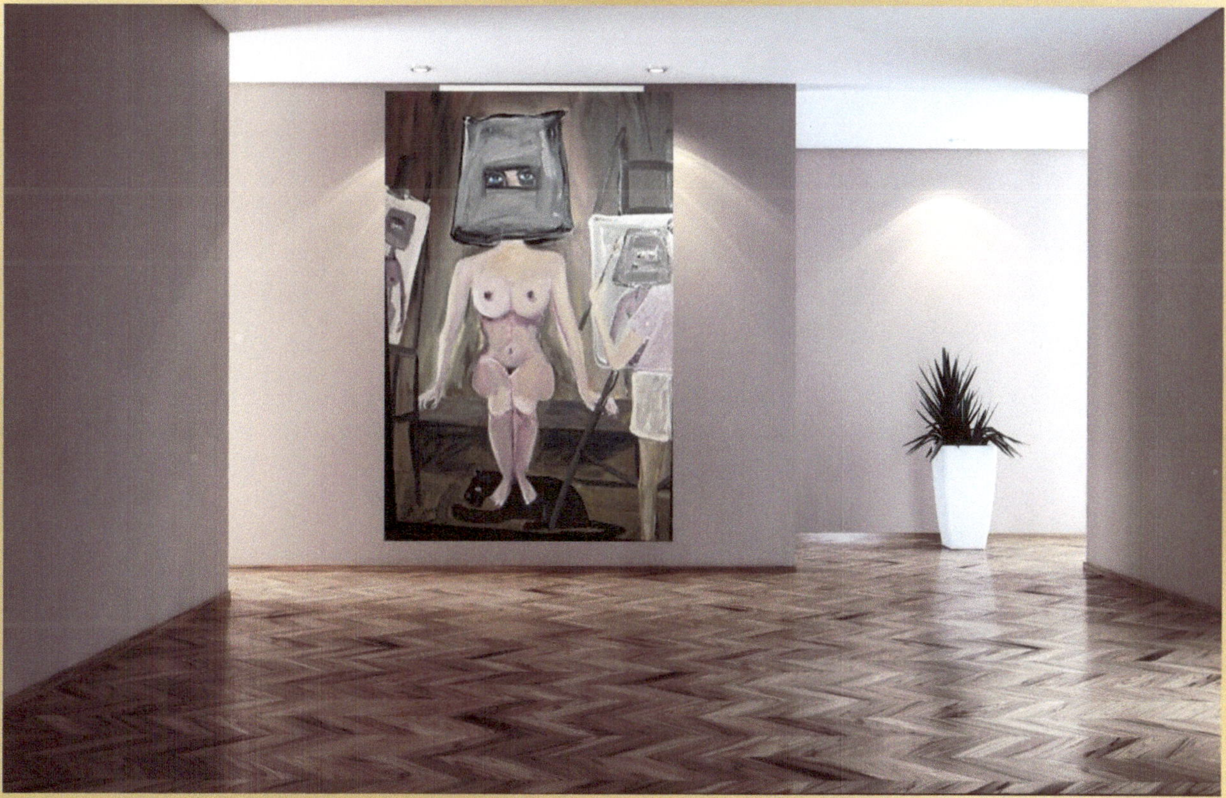

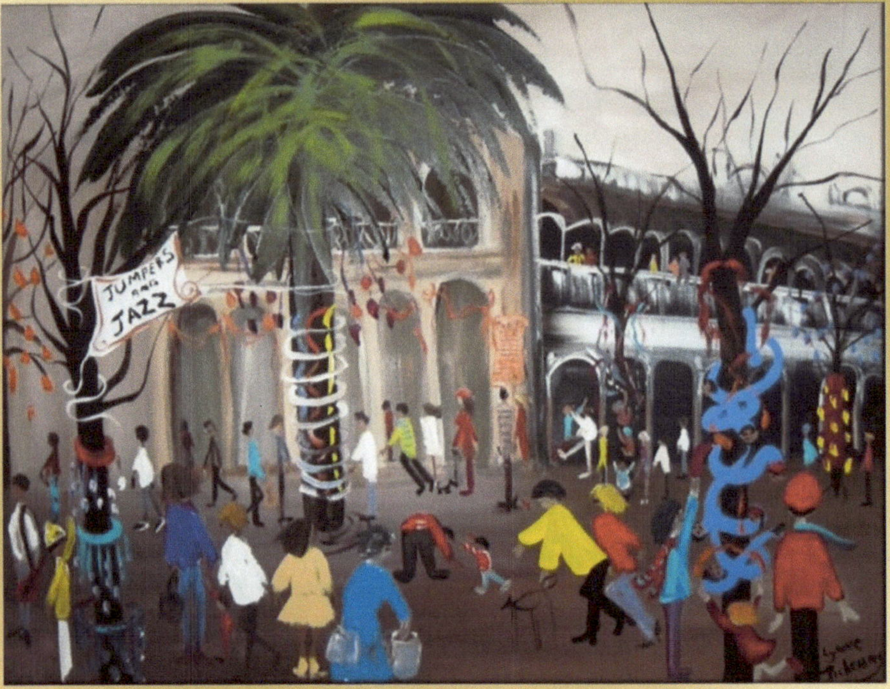
JUMPERS
JAZZ

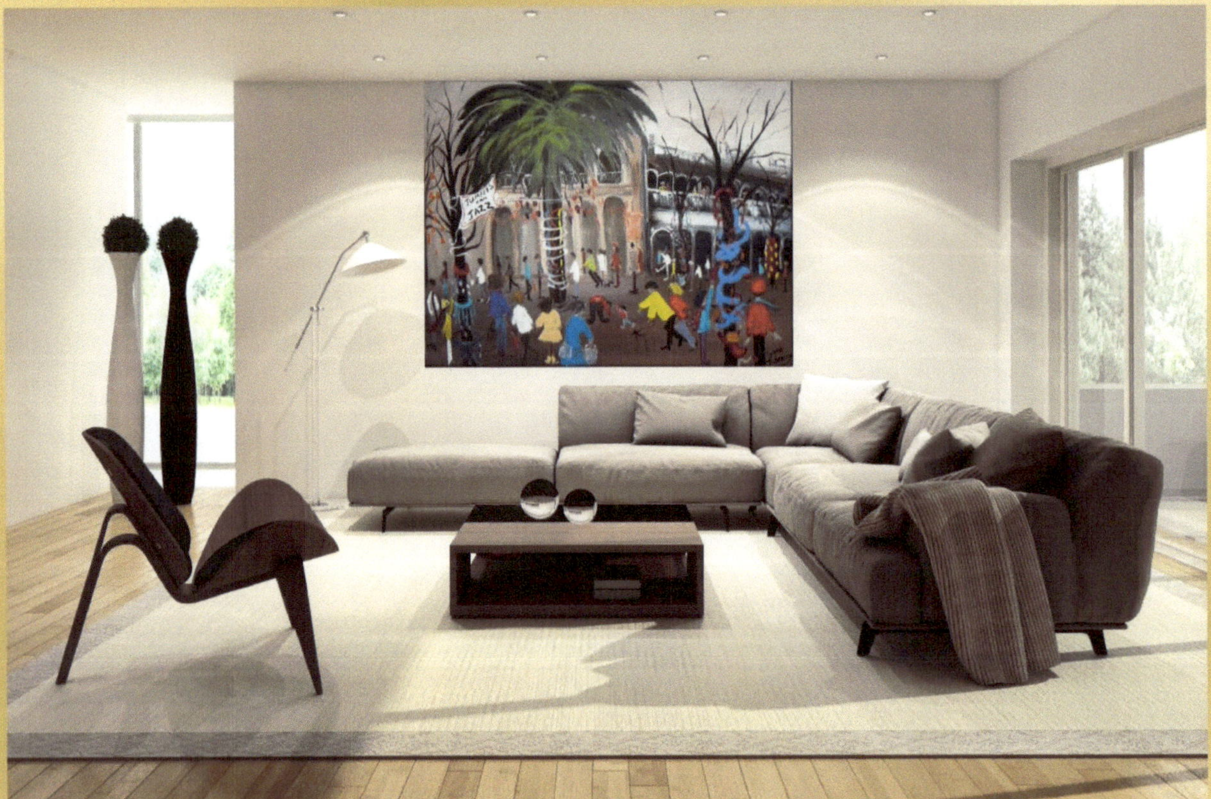

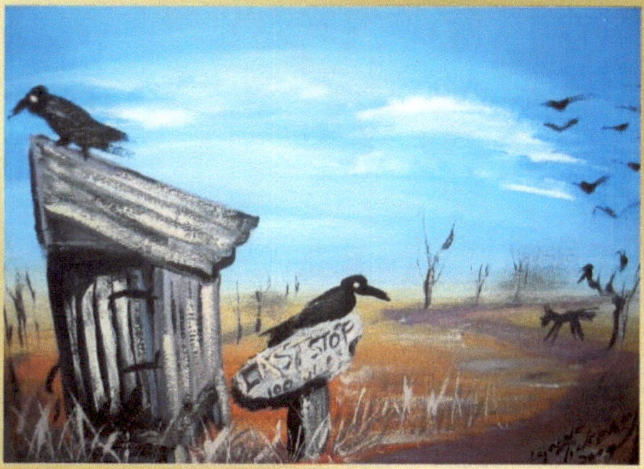

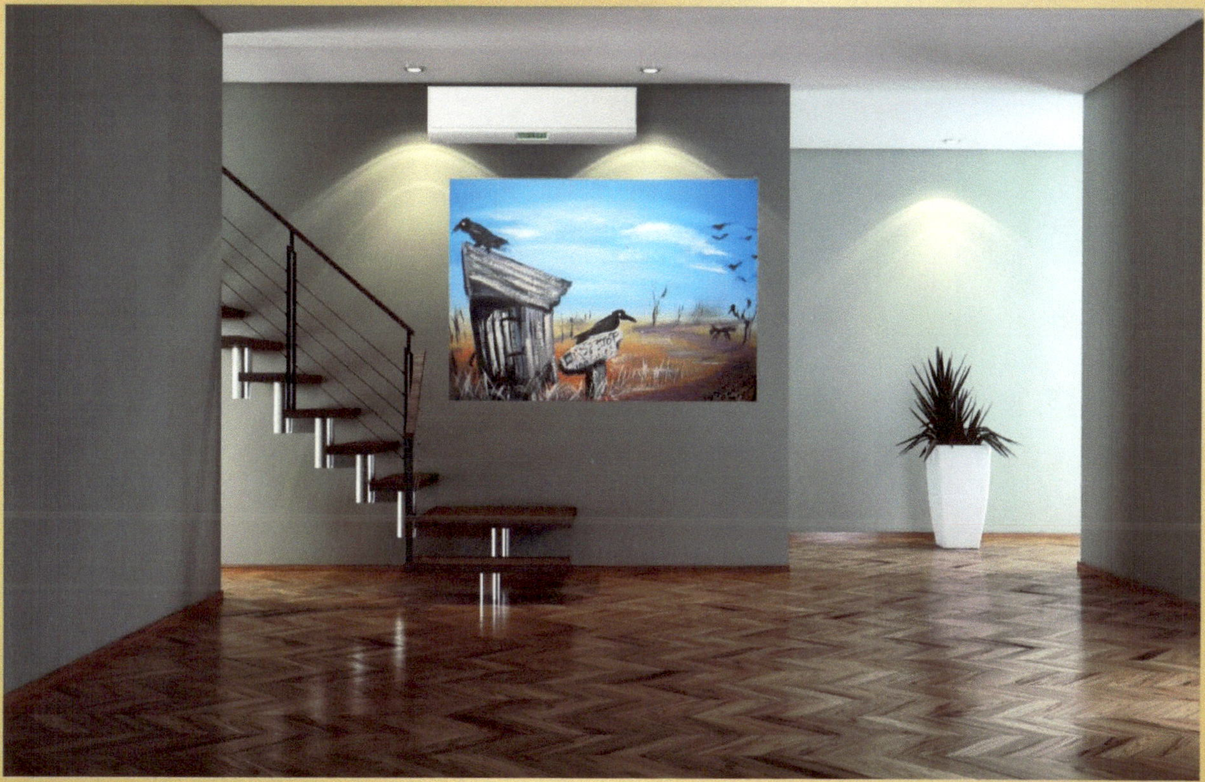

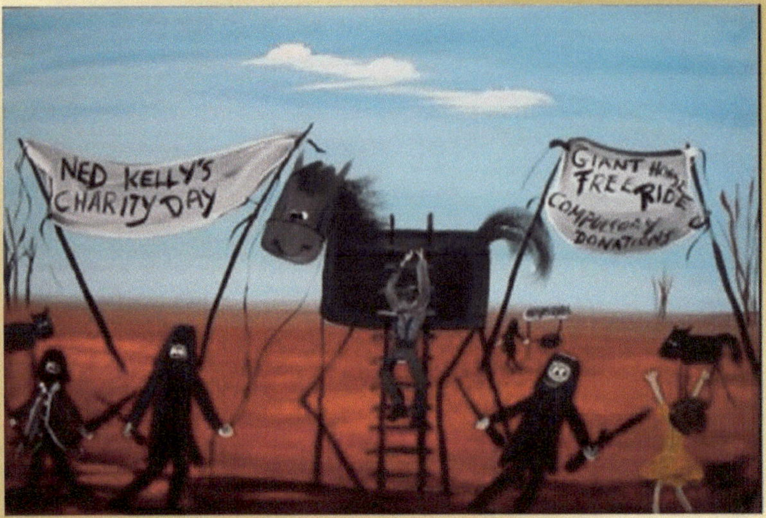
NED KELLY'S CHARITY DAY
GIANT
FREE RIDE
COMPULSORY DONATIONS

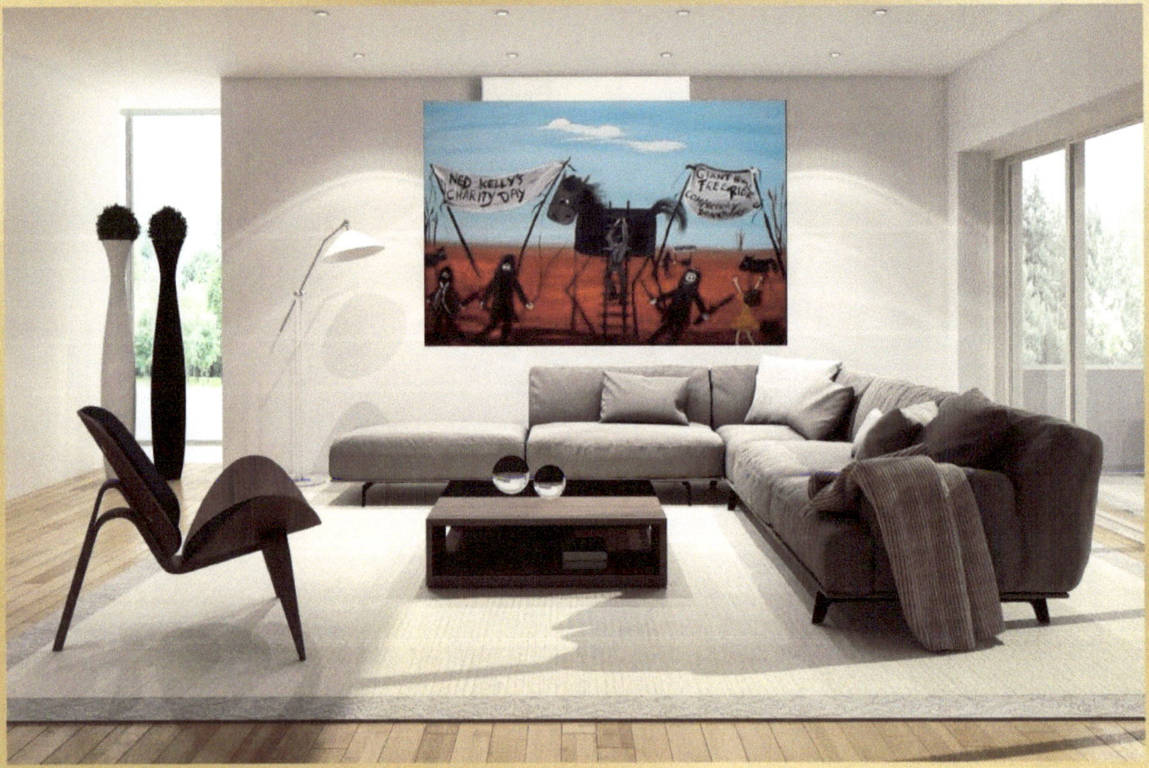

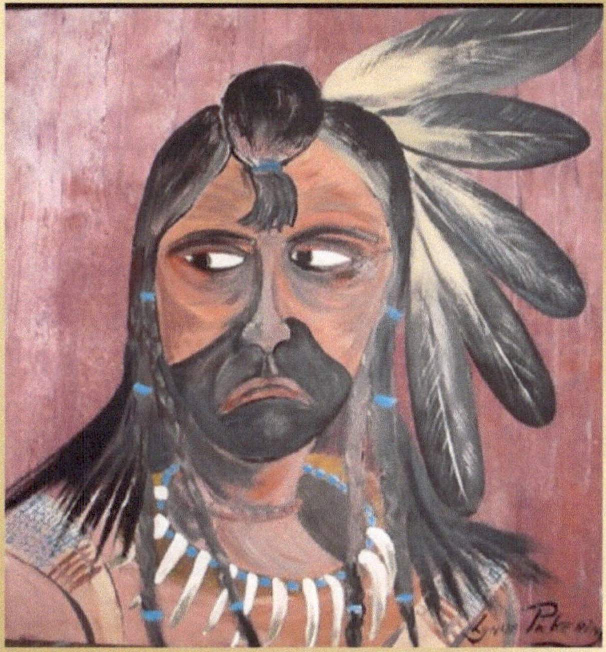

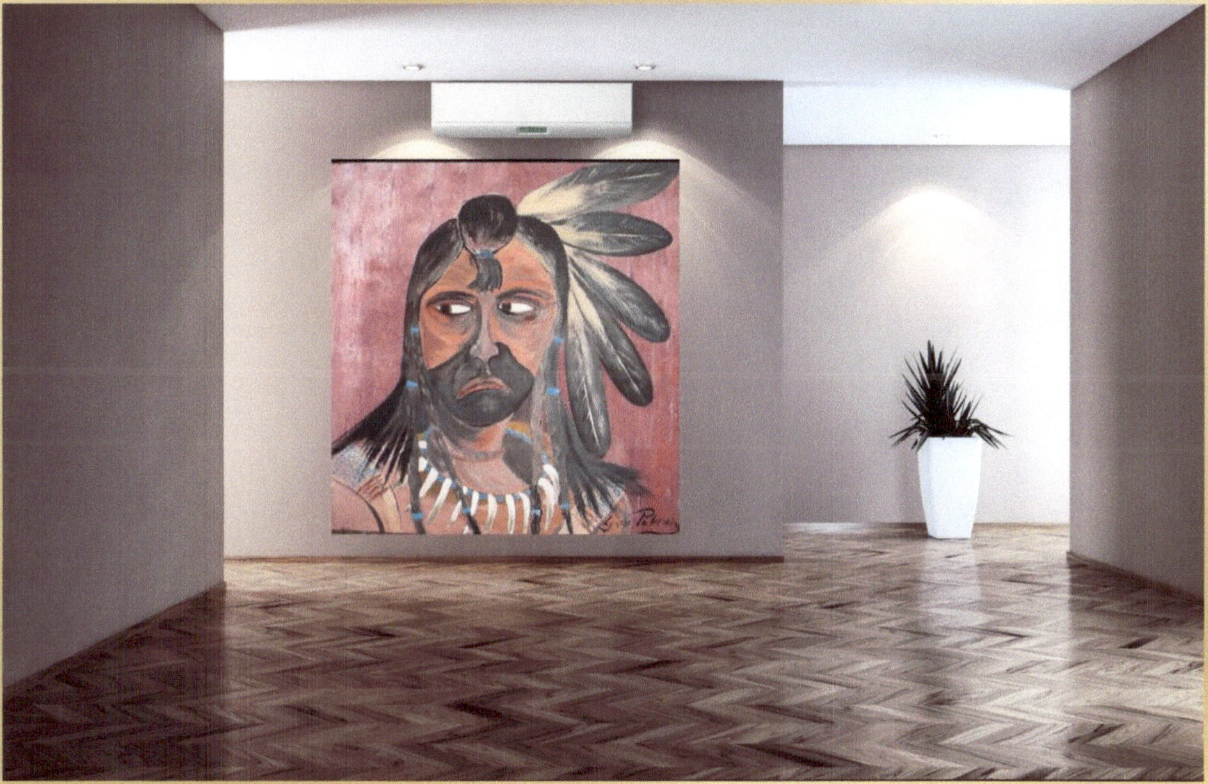

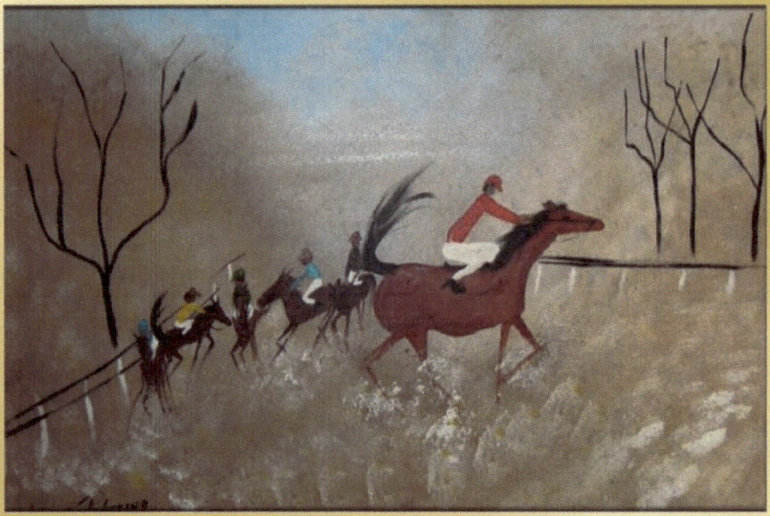

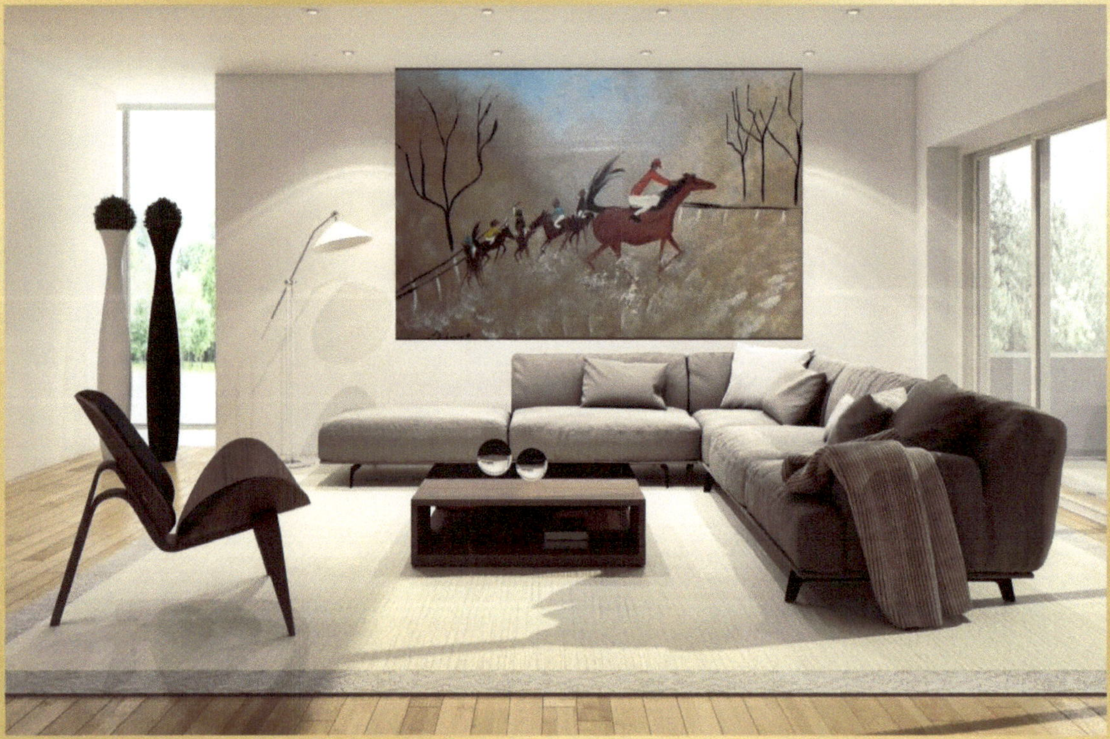

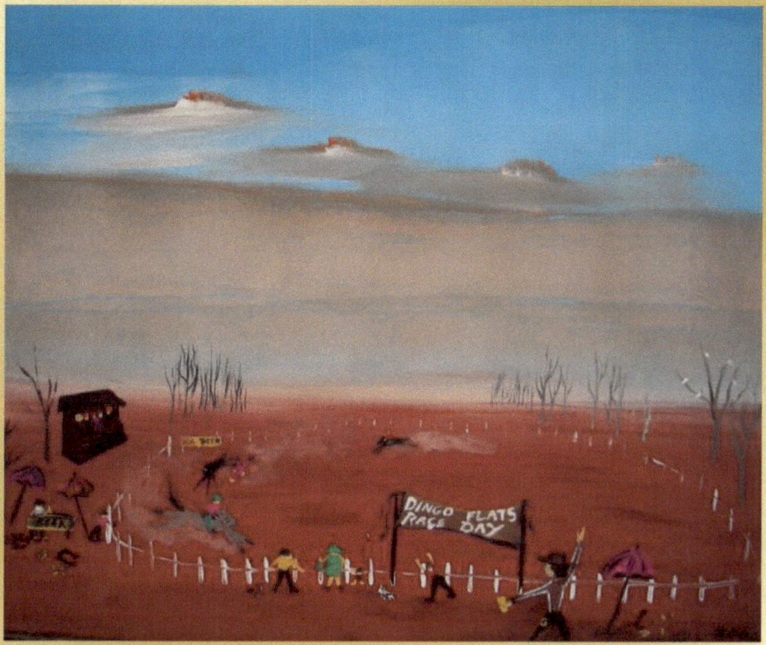
DINGO FLATS
RACE DAY

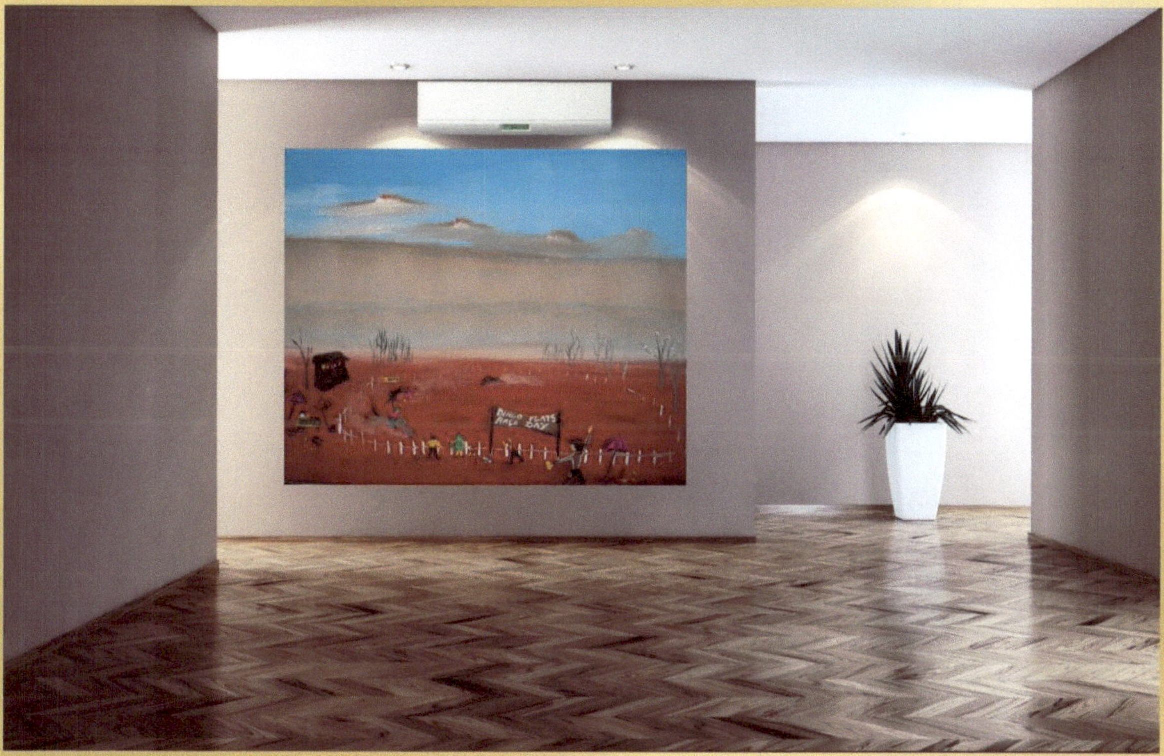

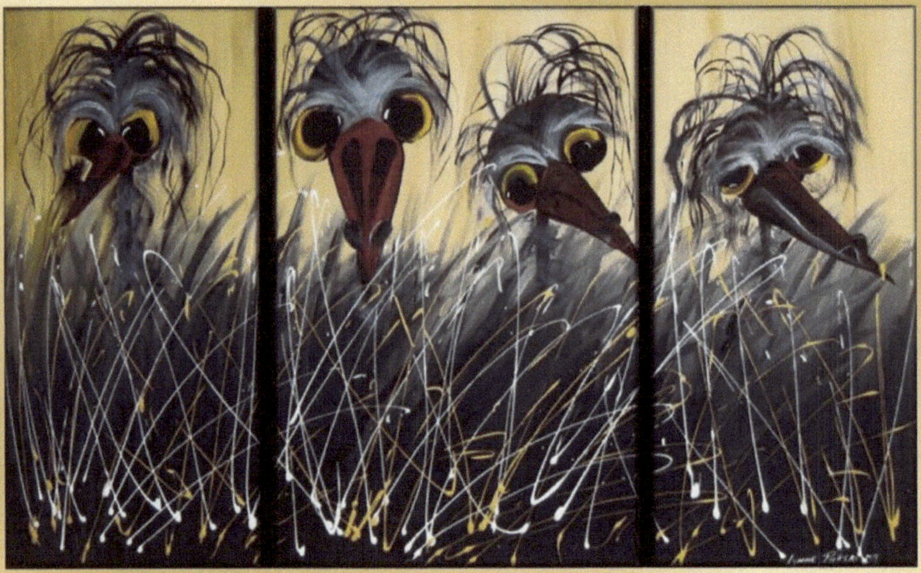

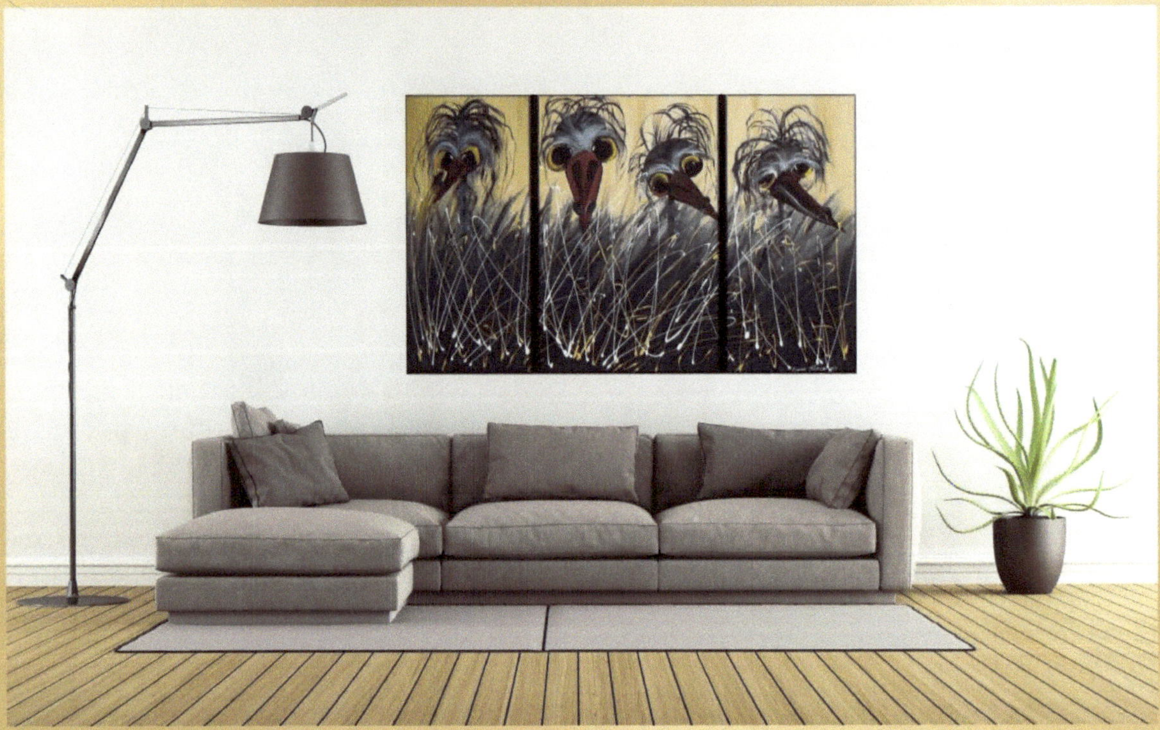

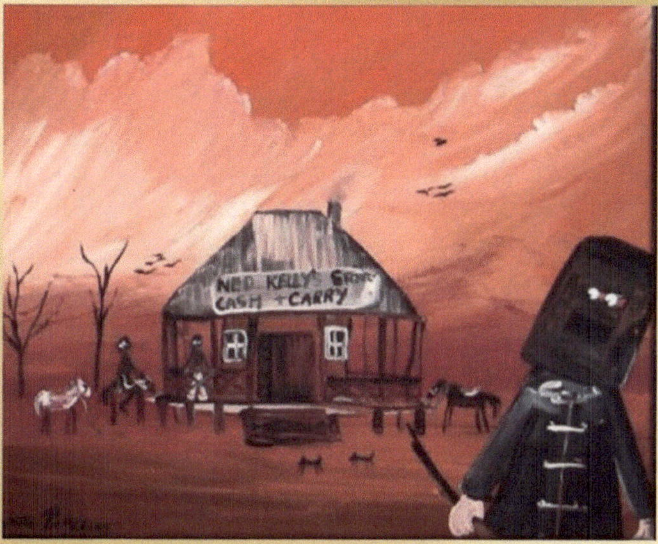
NED KELLY'S
CASH + CARRY

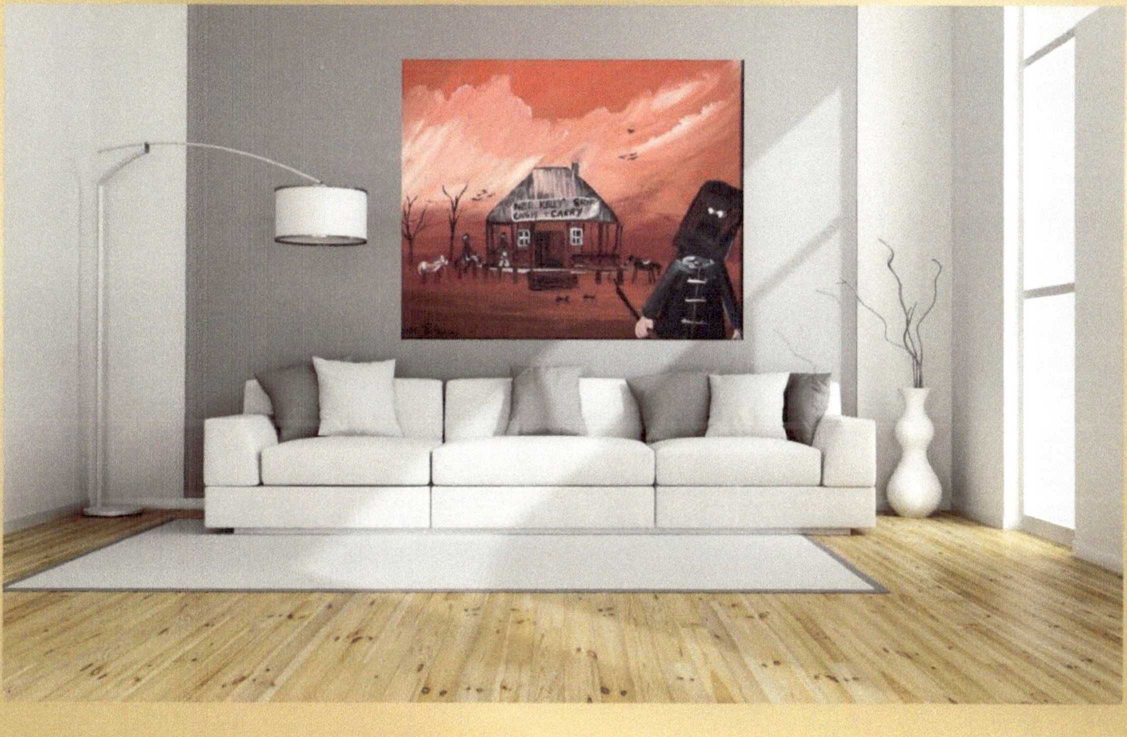

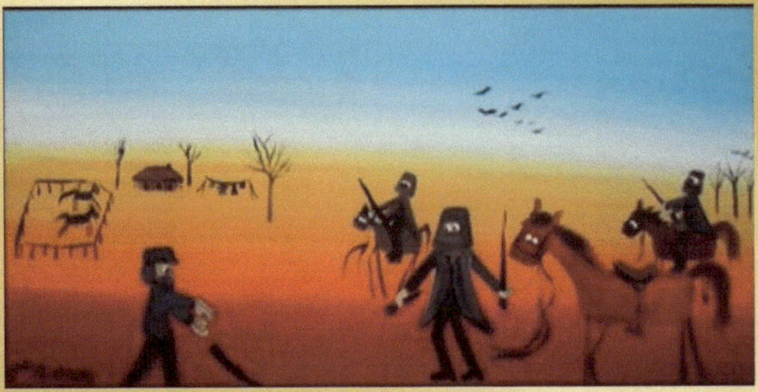

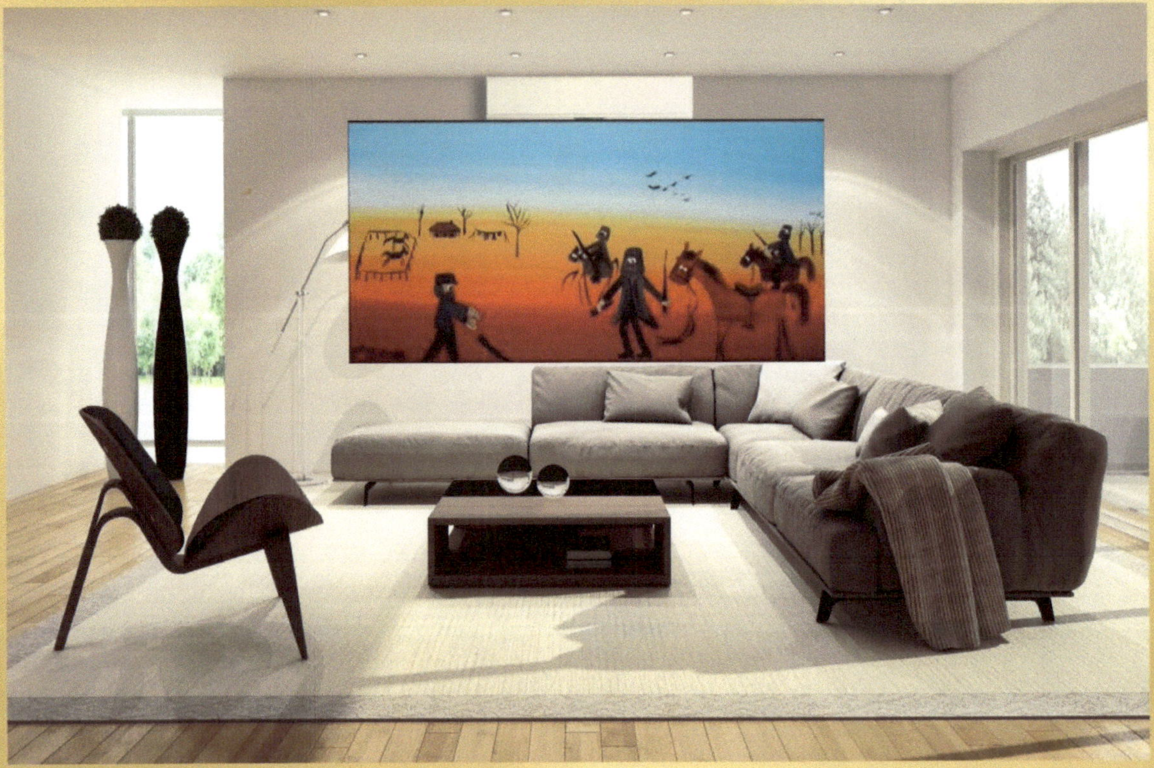

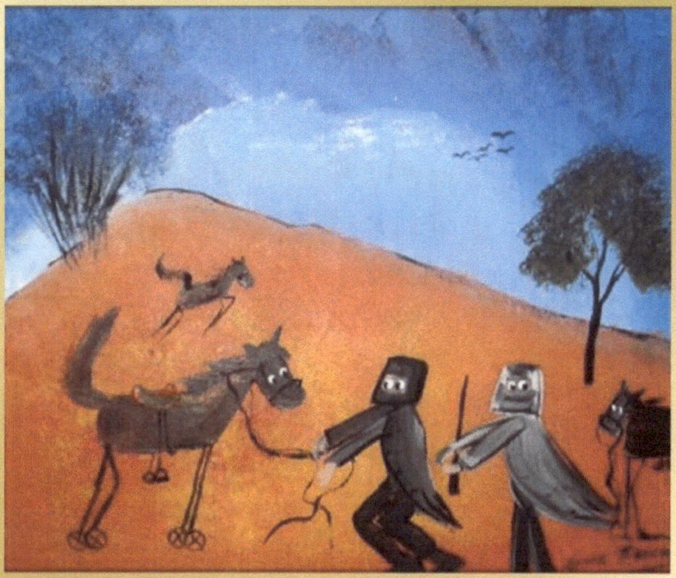

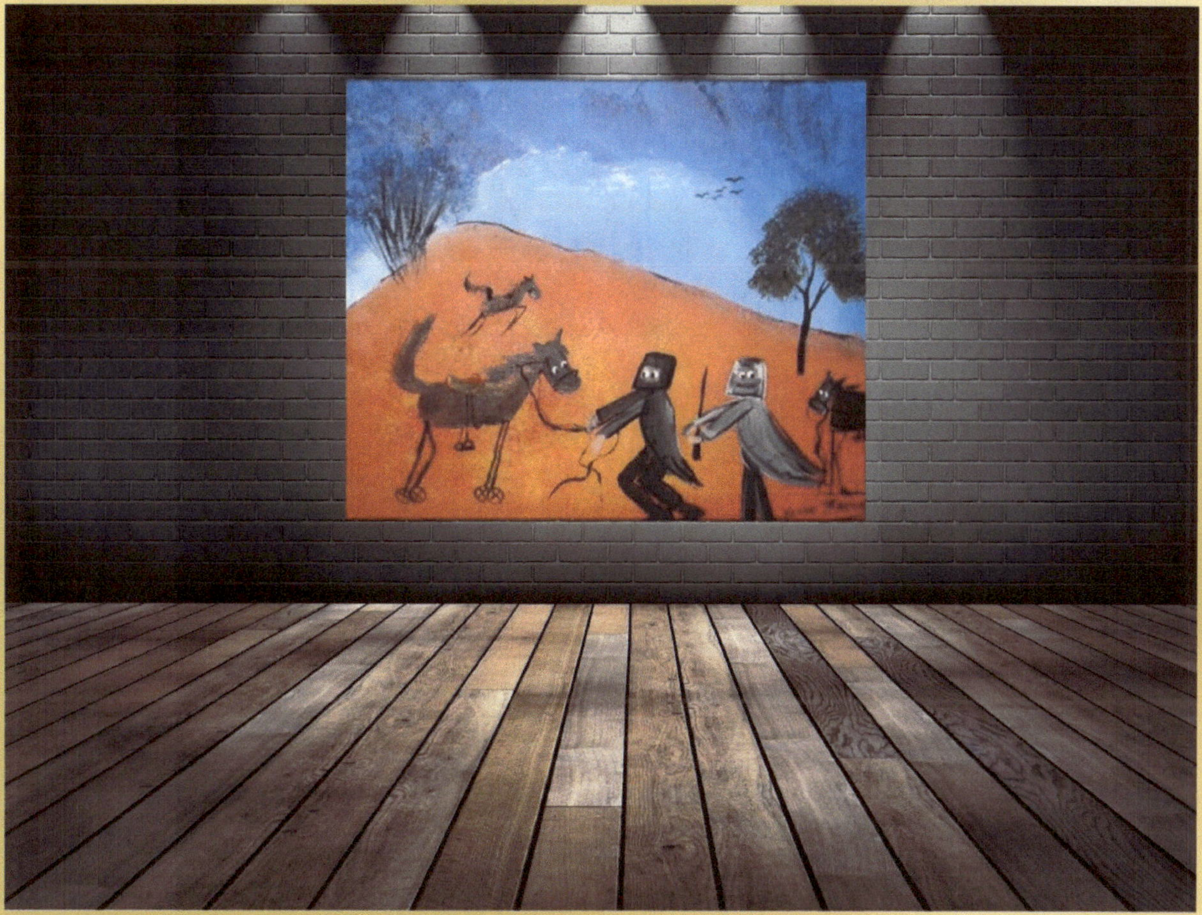

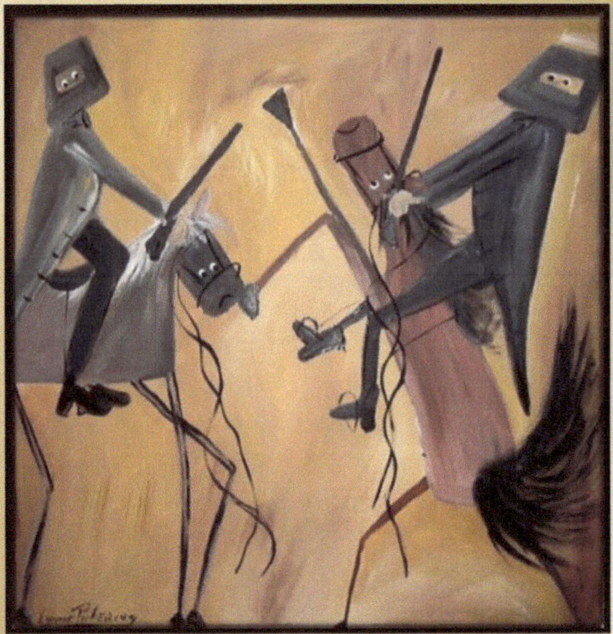

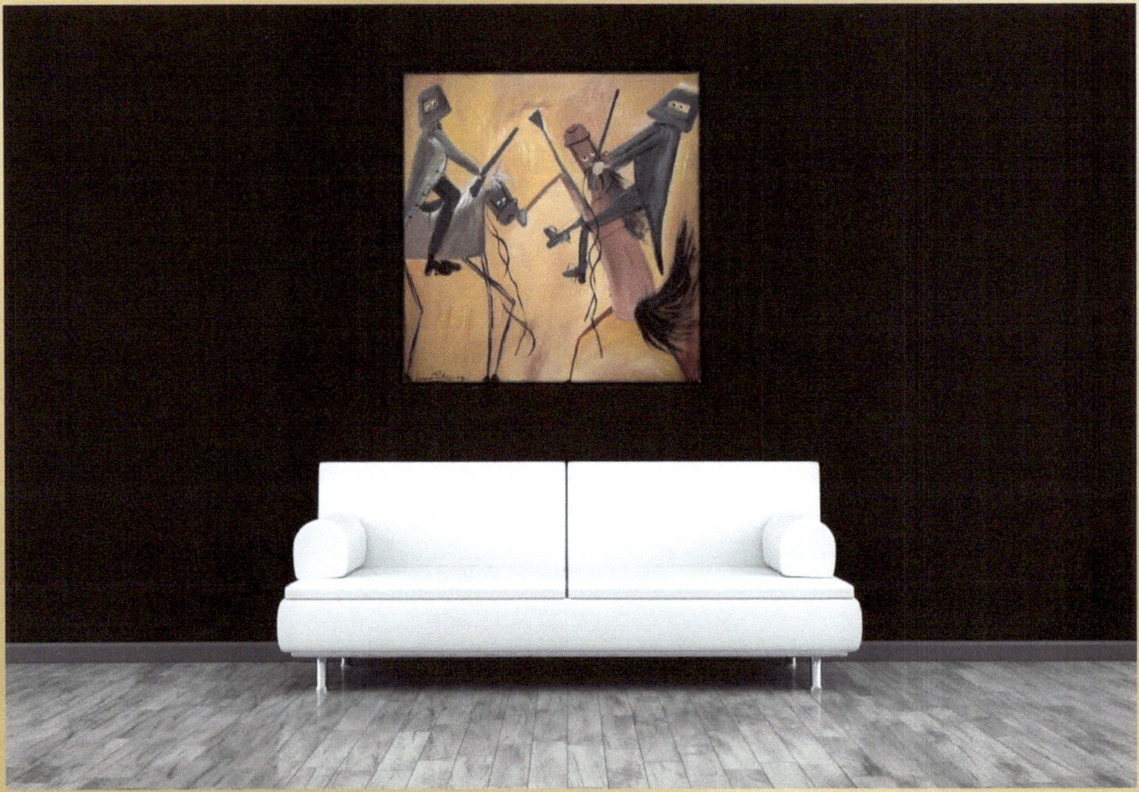

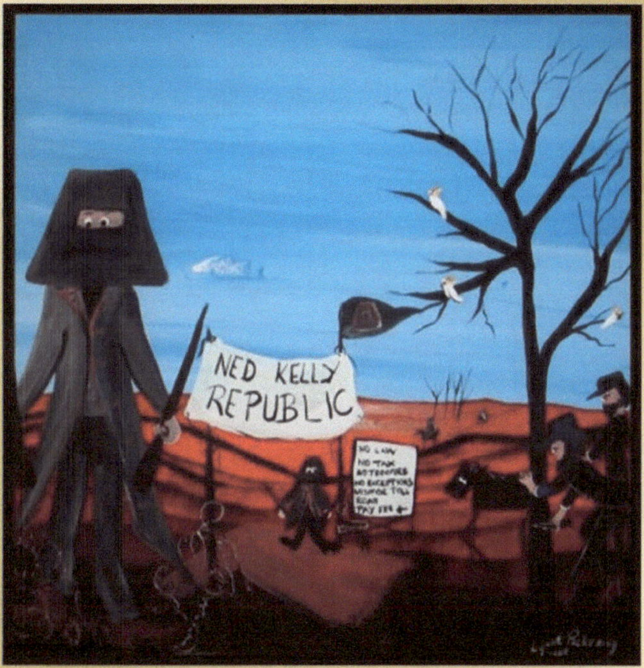
NED KELLY
REPUBLIC
NO LAW
NO TAX

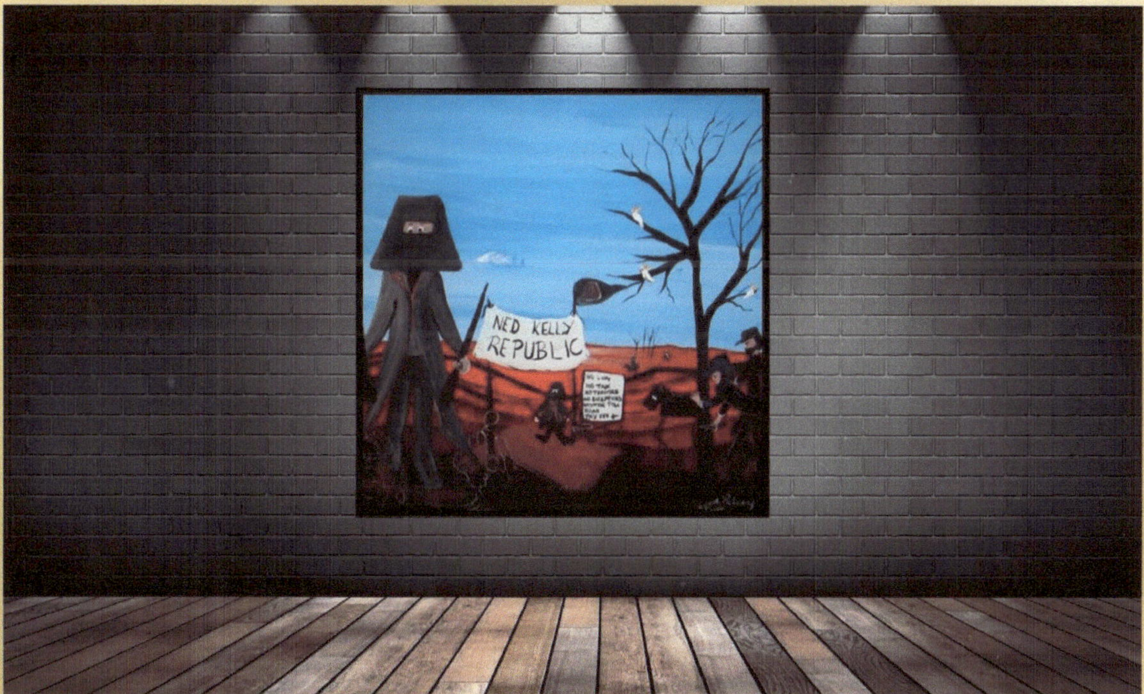
NED KELLY
REPUBLIC

www.ingramcontent.com/pod-product-compliance
Lightning Source LLC
Chambersburg PA
CBHW050838180526
45159CB00004B/1951